A Diary

Reflections & Confessions
of a Mountain Host

Bill Adams
Jackson Hole

A Diary – Reflections & Confessions of a Mountain Host by Bill Adams
Published 2023 by Your Book Angel
Copyright © 2023 Bill Adams
bill.jacksonhole@gmail.com

Printed in the United States
Edited by Keidi Keating
Layout by Rochelle Mensidor

Cover by

ISBN: 979-8-9876155-8-4

Foreword

This book is not fiction. Everything described in this work occurred substantially as written and I take full responsibility for any inaccuracies. The book is dedicated to everyone who is mentioned by name, particularly Lee Ann Inberg-Schuff, my good friends and former law partners, Lowell Martindale and Bob Pisano, and my always-supportive wife of 53 years, Barbara.

I would like to acknowledge the input of Keidi Keating, Your Book Angel, whose initial review and comments inspired me to take a careful look at what I had initially submitted for publication, and ultimately led to important additions and changes resulting in a much improved product. Finally, I wish to thank

Ashanti Falcon, my former assistant of many years who worked with me at my old law firm, for her careful and thoughtful review of the final drafts, her talent at finding errors, and her insightful comments.

Bill Adams, September 2023

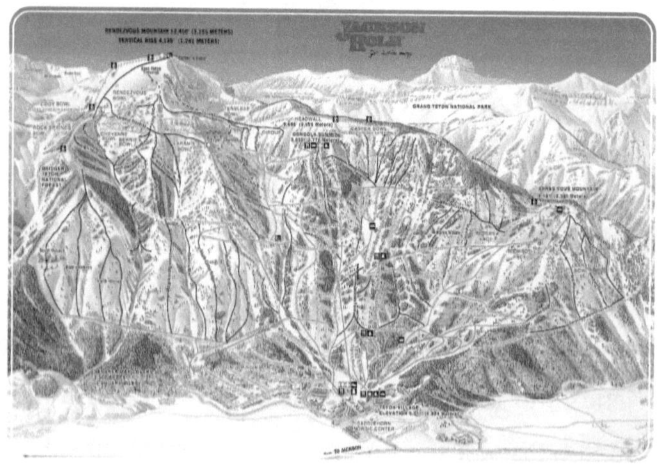

Table of Contents

Prologue

This Diary may only interest those who have been to the Jackson Hole Mountain Resort (JHMR) and are familiar with the mountain and its many runs. For the most part, I added to it daily during the course of the 2005-2006 winter season as I learned how to become a Mountain Host, and it reflects a period of personal growth and discovery. It was then put aside and forgotten until I ran across a copy seventeen years later while cleaning out old files in my office. I read it and decided that, with a little effort, I could transform it into something my friends, and possibly former, present and future Mountain Hosts, as well as visitors to the ski resort, might enjoy reading. This is not intended for the general, non-skiing and snowboarding public.

For those who don't know me well, some background may help put my reflections in context. When the events described below occurred, I was a sixty-six-year-old retired partner at O'Melveny & Myers, a large Los Angeles based law firm with multiple domestic and international offices. I'd spent most of my career working in several west coast offices and the Paris office. My wife, Barbara, and I had owned a partial interest in a Jackson Hole town house at Spring Creek Ranch since 1982 (when it was first developed) and had been skiing at the Mountain Resort for more than twenty years, though only for a week or so each winter. My skiing ability then had been at the mid-intermediate level while skiing groomed runs on clear days. In short, I wasn't an accomplished skier. One other background note should be mentioned because it's part of the story: although I'd had many different types of jobs growing up, I'd never had one that put me in a position to receive a tip.

After retiring from the practice of law in 2000, Barbara and I sold our interest in the town house, built a single family house at Spring Creek Ranch, and moved to Jackson Hole full time in the fall of 2004. While skiing at JHMR that winter, I met several Mountain Hosts—sometimes referred to as "Mountain Ghosts" because they were often hard to find on powder days—and thought it would be a great way to meet locals and become more involved in the community.

My Try-Out to Be a Mountain Host

December 5, 2005 (Monday)

The try-out session was to begin promptly at 9:00 a.m. in the third floor conference room of the JHMR Maintenance and Operations Building (the MOB). We had about six inches of fresh powder overnight and I had been told there would be an orientation meeting, then the candidates would split into small groups and we'd head to the mountain for several hours of skiing with existing Mountain Hosts, apparently to demonstrate our ability to get down the mountain in one piece—and in good humor.

I wanted to succeed, so I planned my approach carefully. I asked Barbara to drop me off in the parking lot at the MOB about fifteen minutes early. I was wearing my ski boots and had put protective rubber pads on the bottoms to make walking easier. I intended to walk through the ground floor with my skis and poles and leave them outside on the mountain side of the building, to be picked up on our way to the slopes. I wanted to avoid the hassle of lugging them upstairs. I was then going to take the elevator to the third floor conference room.

It would have been a good plan, if I'd been able to make it from the parking lot to the mountain side.

Problem was, the bottom floor is like a rabbit warren. I got lost in the maze and never made it to the mountain side. I also slipped on the slick floor and fell on my ass, my skis and poles making a God-awful noise. Thankfully, nobody saw me because, by then, they were all in the conference room.

By the time I arrived with my skis, poles, parka and assorted paraphernalia, I was hot, sweaty and late. I leaned my skis and poles against the wall with a bunch of other skis and found a chair. It felt like the room was ninety degrees. About the time my temperature returned to normal, the head host and her assistant, Lee Ann Inberg-Schuff and Bruce Johnston, assigned the groups and announced we were ready to hit the slopes.

My group consisted of two existing Mountain Hosts and three other (quite young) candidates, two of whom were snowboarders. The only other skier-candidate in my group, Tenley Thompson, told me she had learned to ski before she could walk. Apparently, she'd had trouble learning to walk as a child and her parents put her on skis at the age of two. I tried not to feel intimidated.

I was pleased with the Mountain Hosts they'd assigned to our small group. Ken O'Dell was in his 70s and claimed to be the oldest host on the mountain. The other was Barb Burris, a kind woman who appeared to be in (or near) my age bracket. I thought, *'How bad can this be?'* All I had to do was follow an old guy and a woman "of a certain age," as the French would say. But first, I had to get downstairs in one piece with all my gear.

I grabbed my skis and poles and asked Barb if she would direct me to the elevator. She kindly agreed, and I waited while she put on her gear. It was so warm in the building that I avoided putting my helmet and gloves on until after we got outside.

We made it down the elevator without incident, and while Barb and the others headed to the bottom of the Teewinot lift to meet up with Ken, I fumbled with my gear. Finally, I was ready, and even though the others had already departed, I was confident I could catch them before they started up the mountain.

Then I tried to step into my bindings—nothing. I couldn't fit my boots into them. They looked like my skis, but the bindings were too small. I thought I picked up the wrong pair of skis and some other candidate had taken mine. That's when I saw Dede Burnstine, one of the other Mountain Hosts leading her troupe to the lift. I quickly explained my problem, and she radioed *all* the other hosts and announced that Bill had picked up the wrong pair of skis. Dede said someone would take care of the situation, and she took off to rejoin her group.

I waited. Then I tried several more times to fit my boots into the bindings, just in case. One finally went in. It was then that I discovered I had not removed the protective rubber pads from my boots! They *were* my skis after all.

So far, it had not been an excellent day.

Ken, Barb and my fellow candidates had already taken the Teewinot Quad Chair by the time I arrived, so having no option other than to make the best of the situation or bail from the program—I headed up by myself. Fortunately, I found my group patiently waiting for me at the bottom of the Après Vous Quad Chair.

By the time the lift deposited us at the top of AV, I had stopped hyperventilating.

We took a run, and I was beginning to feel okay when our leader, Ken, told us we would head over to Casper. Still no problem I thought, '*Casper is a piece of cake.'* So, off we went. We came down Sleeping Indian and started to swing back to lower AV. That's when I got an inkling of what was to come.

The old guy was a maniac on telemark skis. And worse, he liked to go off the groomed trails.

We arrived at the bottom and took the Bridger Gondola up the mountain. At the top, Ken said he wanted to see how well we could handle powder. So, off he went down Ranger, an ungroomed black run, and through the woods. The first time Ken fell, I knew I was in trouble. The second time I saw him fall I knew I wanted to get back to the groomed runs. It was about then that I almost took out Barb, who'd made the mistake of getting in front of me. I was having difficulty in the powder and Barb, being both kind and perceptive, suggested we ski through a stand of trees over to the upper, double blue and groomed Sundance run and meet up with the others further down the mountain.

We met the others on the traverse to Thunder. Fortunately, the Thunder lift was closed, so we instead headed to the bottom via lower Gros Ventre.

All in all, I had an awful time. My plan had failed. I'd gotten all hot and bothered and had fallen twice, something I almost never do (once on AV and a second time on Sundance after making it through the trees with Barb). My only solace was something Ken had said before our first run, "The best skiers are usually not the best Mountain Hosts." I guess that's because they may be more interested in skiing than hosting. I'm not sure that's true, but I was happy to find comfort wherever I could.

I returned home and told Barbara what had happened. After she stopped laughing, I was finally able to see the humor in what had occurred. It was quite an experience.

When Lee Ann called the next day to let me know their decision, I was quite surprised to learn I had been selected as a host. I concluded it can only improve from here.

Orientation

December 8 (Thursday)

Today was our orientation meeting. There was no skiing, so I was relatively safe. Instead, we met in the conference room and listened to presentations by Lee Ann, her assistant, Bruce, and a host (pardon the pun) of others, including the Director of Communications for JHMR, the head of Human Resources, the benefits person, the head of safety, the head of the Ski Patrol and assorted others. We also were given several forms to fill out and sign, including a self-styled contract regarding the host's commitment to JHMR and its obligations to the hosts, including, among other things, providing a uniform.

During the orientation, Lee Ann told us JHMR had decided to make a real push to improve guest relations this year. The term assigned to the effort was "passionate purpose," (*really?*) and the Mountain Host program will be an important part of the passionate purpose effort. As a consequence, they'd decided to almost double the number of hosts by adding an additional twenty or so people. I suspect that was, at least in part, the reason why I made it through the try-outs. Sometimes circumstances, a smile and friendly demeanor can be more important than the skill to back it up.

That was the good news. The bad news was JHMR didn't make its decision to augment its corps of hosts until sometime last summer, several months after the order for Mountain Host uniforms had been placed with the supplier, Marmot. As Lee Ann explained it, "We have more hosts than uniforms to put them in." The only solution was to require the new hosts to share uniforms.

Of course, the first question any sane person would ask is, "What does the uniform consist of?"

You start with the ski pants, then add a wind shirt, a vest or light jacket, and finally an outer shell (we 'layer' in Jackson Hole).

I'm not sure how all this will shake out, but I'll wait and see.

During the orientation meeting each new host was assigned the days he or she is required to be on the mountain. Each has committed to work two full days every week. Fortunately, I was given my first choice of Tuesday and Thursday. If you miss a day, for any reason, it must be made up. There are *no* exceptions. I'm already committed to a trip in late February that would cause me to miss three days, but figure I have time to find someone to switch days with me. Nonetheless, I took note of the rule.

Lee Ann took us through the Mountain Host Handbook which includes, among other things, a list of the various host assignments and a discussion of their duties. I discovered there's a lot more to this job than I had imagined. I'm actually quite concerned about seeing a skier with an injury in rough terrain. I could always call the Ski Patrol, but they expect the host to first get to the skier, make sure he or she is protected from others coming down the mountain, and assess the situation (including the nature of the injury, the person's approximate age, name, sex and condition). That could be difficult while peering over the edge of a catwalk at someone half buried in snow ten or twenty yards down a steep slope. Somehow I don't think we are only expected to help those fortunate enough to be injured on a groomed slope.

To address that concern, I've decided to sign up for the Ski & Race Camp program starting this Sunday. It's a six-day program, and I will either have to miss hosting or miss Race Camp on Tuesday and Thursday. One of the new hosts, Lynnie Hollbacher, has agreed to take my shift on Tuesday (the first day I'm supposed to work as a host), and I've decided to host on Thursday and skip Ski & Race Camp that day.

I'm told by those who've attended in the past that your level of skiing after the camp is about what it would ordinarily be mid-season without attending. If that will help me get to injured skiers in rough terrain, it'll be worth it.

I didn't ski after the orientation. Instead, I tried to organize my locker, locate the room to store my skis and figure out the rabbit warren maze in the MOB, particularly the location of the elevator to the ground floor. I'm happy I didn't get lost, fall on my ass or otherwise make a fool of myself.

The fearless leader of the Jackson Hole Mountain Hosts, Lee Ann Inberg-Schuff.

Pre-Hosting

December 9 (Friday)

I now have an All Mountain Pass that allows me to ski at any time, free of charge, so I decided to head to Teton Village and take a few runs. I also wanted to buy a pair of Marmot ski pants and a wind shirt so I wouldn't have to share those items. One of the benefits of being a host is a 20% discount on ski equipment. I got the pants but struck out in finding a wind shirt (it has to be black).

After buying my pants, I hiked up the hill to the MOB to get my skis and headed up the mountain as a "host-to-be." It felt great, even though I wasn't wearing a Mountain Host uniform (borrowed or otherwise). Today was a free ski day, and I wanted to enjoy it before facing the challenges of Ski & Race Camp or hosting.

It occurred to me, however, that this hiking business could get old awfully fast. The Mountain Host office, meeting room and lockers are in the MOB, located about two hundred yards *up* the beginner's slope. Meaning, I'll have to walk up and back every day I'm at the mountain. I'm not excited about hiking in the snow and I'd like to figure out some way to avoid it.*

As you face the mountain the in-bound terrain at JHMR runs north-south, with the Après View lift on the far right, or north end, and the Sublette lift on the far left. There are expert runs off all upper mountain lifts, but as a general rule the terrain becomes more difficult as you move from north to south. As in all ski resorts, there are colored trail markings with green for easier, blue

---

* *I finally solved the hiking problem in 2009 by becoming a member of Shooting Star Country Club. They provided a shuttle service for me from the Club to the MOB.*

for intermediate, black diamond for advanced or most difficult, and on some mountains, a yellow or double black diamond marking for expert skiers. JHMR, however, differs from most other ski resorts. In addition to the traditional trail markings, they have added a double blue which is equivalent to a black diamond on most mountains, a single black diamond is equivalent to expert elsewhere, and a double black diamond is for the insane skier. When referring to its trail designations, JHMR has the following warning on its Mountain Map & Guide: "This is a system specific to Jackson Hole and does not reflect the same degree of difficulty as similarly rated trails at other ski areas."

As a conscientious host-to-be, I decided to start at AV and make my way south across the mountain to check out the groomed terrain—and, of course, keep my eye out for skiers in trouble. While I was taking the Thunder lift to the top, I noticed that much of the terrain heading over to the Sublette Quad Chair has rather large moguls. I don't like moguls. But I did want to take the Sublette lift, so I headed in that direction.

That's when I had my very first (unofficial) hosting experience.

As I was skiing down Egg Carton toward the trail divide between the double blue groomed Grand run on skiers right and the double blue, but ungroomed and mogul-strewn Gannet run to the left, I came across a couple that was quite clearly uncomfortable with the terrain. The fellow would ski for ten yards or so and fall, and the woman had decided they should take the left fork heading for Gannet. At that point I felt there was a hosting opportunity. I approached them and offered to lead them on an easier route back across the mountain to the bottom of AV. They accepted and we headed down Grand.

As I had been instructed by Lee Ann and Bruce, I stopped every forty yards or so to be sure the couple was still with me. We chatted, and I learned the man, Jonathan Shapiro, had graduated from Yale law school, worked as a public prosecutor in Los Angeles and had briefly worked in my old law firm. He'd left to write speeches for Lieutenant Governor Bustamante of California and started writing scripts for television, including "The Practice." His wife, Betsy, writes screen plays.

The only problem they had was starting with the gondola. Rather than going to the right, or north side of the mountain, they'd decided to head up the center. In fact, by making their way south they seem to have made all the wrong decisions about what route to take. It's not uncommon for many first time visitors to put themselves in jeopardy without first inquiring about which lift to take, as many newcomers to JHMR don't think about the altitude and how important it is to stay hydrated, how easy it is to become exhausted after a too strenuous first day, and the need to learn about the mountain and how its trail markings may differ from that of other ski resorts. As a consequence, many first time visitors start by taking the most convenient lift, which is usually the gondola.

I'll talk to the concierge at Spring Creek Ranch and let her know the Mountain Hosts will give a free two-hour complementary tour of the mountain to any group wishing it, so long as they're ready to start by 9:30 a.m. Though I wonder if that's too early for those heading up the mountain the first skiing day after their arrival. It might be more effective to have two tours starting from the base of the mountain, one at 9:30 a.m. and the other an hour later.

That's something I may suggest to our fearless leader, Lee Ann.

Ski & Race Camp

December 11 to 16 (Sunday through Friday)

I started Ski & Race Camp on Sunday. The camp runs from 9:00 a.m. to 3:30 p.m. They break everyone into relatively small groups of seven or so skiers having generally the same ability. During the course of the six days, there are three instructors per group, each for two days. Perhaps it was the luck of the draw, but our group appeared to have three of the best and most experienced ski instructors at JHMR.

Our first instructor was Renny Burke. Next, we had Bruce Keller. And finally, for the real racing phase, we had an instructor known to us only by one name, Theo. In our group, the youngest participant, Jay Grabow, was from Rawlings. The fastest was Ray Johnson from California. In between, we had six men with an *average* age of sixty-seven. Included in my group were Peter Ordway, Brent Backman, John Davies, Joel Berman and Bill Iams.*

I learned a lot during the course of the six days, not the least of which that I may be the only person in the universe (or in Jackson Hole) who can ski reasonably well but is really uncomfortable once venturing off the groomed trails. I've got to work on this part of my "game."

We had an actual NASTAR race on the sixth day down a fairly challenging Giant Slalom course set up on the Upper Werner and Moran runs at Après Vous. The course had two parallel sets of gates: one green, the other yellow. The idea was to have two skiers leave the starting gates at the same time and race each other down the course. Each skier had two runs, one on each of the two sets of gates. Your

____

* *Joel Berman was a long-time Mountain Host, and Bill Iams was to become a host several years later.*

opportunity to win a NASTAR medal was based on your time on each of the two runs and on the combined score, assuming you weren't disqualified on either of the runs.

The first two skiers to go were Tommy Moe—the downhill gold medal winner at Lillehammer eleven years ago—racing against his wife, Megan Gerety, a World Cup winner. Their job was to set the pace. Their time on each set of gates was, in effect, the "gold standard" against which all other skiers were to be judged. Each skier is given a handicap based on a number of factors, including prior experience, age and the like. Since I'd never skied around gates, and was somewhat advanced in age, I presumed I would have a significant handicap. Or so I hoped.

I was one of the first two camp participants to run the course. I was right behind Megan (who, incidentally, beat her husband). Well, right behind is a bit of an overstatement. By the time I finished my run, she had unbuckled her boots and had almost finished her cappuccino. I did have a big advantage in following her, however. I had a relatively fresh course and had watched her approach to the first gate. During gate training in Ski & Race Camp you learn pretty quickly that if you round the first gate at the wrong angle, you'll spend the rest of the course trying to get back on the right line and your time will suffer.

I made both runs without a DQ and was happy to have survived without mishap. I also was pleased that I'd skied well enough to win a bronze NASTAR medal. Not bad for an old dude—and a novice, at that.

Everyone in our group won a medal (one of only three groups to achieve that distinction). All of us received a bronze medal except for Ray Johnson and Joel Berman, both of whom earned silver. That will be my goal next year.

A goal achieved: Bill running the gates at the end of Ski & Race Camp a year later, in December 2006, on his way to a silver NASTAR medal.

Hosting

December 15 (Thursday)

Today was my first day hosting. I had to take today off from Ski & Race Camp to host. If I'd taken the entire first week off of work, I feared being viewed as a potential problem host by Lee Ann. In addition, I didn't want to start my duties in a catch up mode.

There's always an 8:00 a.m. meeting in the MOB to start the day. Lee Ann gives the day's assignments and discusses other pending issues. She has a unique way of expressing herself. She is unscripted, politically incorrect, graphic and at times hilarious. I've concluded you never want to miss her morning briefing.

Just before the meeting, she gave me a Mountain Host parka and said I wouldn't have to share it. I'm not sure, but I think they split up the inner shells and the parkas so everyone has his or her own uniform. I was grateful, so I didn't ask. I'll deal with the warm days when they come. Now, at least, I look like a host—except that the name tags for the new hosts haven't yet arrived.

Each host (for that matter, each employee at JHMR) has a name tag that identifies the person's home town. Specifically, where they come from, not where they currently reside. The notion appears to be that showing a home town other than Jackson Hole can be an ice breaker with visitors while riding a chair lift or the gondola. I had two choices: Newport Beach, California or Paris, France. We have homes in both places. I chose the former, in part because of the often negative reaction some Americans have about the French these days, and I'm interested in provoking a warm response, not an icy one.

Rory McKernan, a good looking guy Bruce referred to as "Hollywood," Susanne Knighton, and I were given a 'mock' tour by Tim Filla, a second year host. The complementary tour is led by a Mountain Host. It is supposed to be limited to intermediate, groomed terrain, and begins at AV. At the bottom of the run you take the Togwotee Pass Traverse over to Casper. From there you head to the bottom of the mountain via lower Sundance Gully, and then take the gondola. Once at the top, if the skiers are capable, you head over to Thunder and on to Sublette. The tour generally takes two hours.

Once our group got to the top of the gondola, we headed back down to pick up the tram. Tim apparently decided to take us on the route we'd follow from the top of Rendezvous Bowl if we were to give a complementary tour from that point (generally given once an hour during the day by a tram host for those wanting to find the easiest way down from the "Top of the World"). He told us a tram ride to the top of Rendezvous Bowl is not part of the normal mountain tour.

It was about 1:15 p.m. when we finished skiing the bowl, and Tim said I was free to break off and rejoin my Race Camp group for the remainder of the day. I headed for the MOB to change out of my Mountain Host jacket since Lee Ann made it clear the hosts can't engage in free skiing while in uniform.

Around 2:00 p.m. I met up with my group on AV, just above the race course that had already been set up. Apparently, I hadn't missed much since the group spent the morning with Theo (our third instructor) skiing as fast as they could all over the mountain—they had not yet started gate training. After I arrived, we took a couple runs with Theo and then were joined by Tommy Moe for gate training.*

December 20 (Tuesday)

This was my first real day hosting without a chaperone. My assignment was with Nick Centrella, a fellow newbie. We had Après Vous in the morning and Thunder in the afternoon. No problem; it was

---

* *It was fortunate I was able to rejoin my group on Thursday because the gate training proved to be invaluable to me the next day when all camp participants had to run the gates, racing for a NASTAR medal.*

a clear day, the slopes were well groomed, and I felt good, having almost six full days of Ski & Race Camp under my belt.

Each host carries a radio and is able to tune it into communications among members of various departments on the mountain, including Mountain Hosts, Ski Patrol, Mountain Station, Ski School, Maintenance and the like. The first host to ski down a run in the morning and in the afternoon is supposed to give a general skiing report on the host channel. I was the first host to ski down AV and gave my report at the bottom of the run. I have to admit, I rehearsed it several times before pressing the button on the radio, and it went well. I had passed my first test.

I also dispensed my first quasi medical advice to a young couple on AV. It was their first day. They were from New York City, and she was in obvious pain. She had cramps in her foot, so I suggested she hydrate pointing out the significant change in altitude. Her husband had some Gatorade in his backpack, and it seemed to do the trick.

The day was uneventful until I heard on the radio a call from Tenley, my fellow host candidate who'd learned to ski before she learned to walk. She asked Lee Ann to come to the bottom of Paint Brush, an expert run on Thunder. I learned later that Tenley had an unfortunate encounter with a boulder and tore her ACL near the base in an area of the run known by the locals as "Toilet Bowl." She's a gutsy gal, and I wasn't surprised to learn that she had apologized to Lee Ann for the injury and not being able to continue as a host.

In the afternoon, I was assigned to Thunder and purposely stayed away from Paint Brush and Toilet Bowl.

The day concluded without further incident, and I spent the last forty-five minutes or so on Aloha duty at the bottom of the mountain. Mountain Hosts have Meet & Greet duty in the morning and Aloha in the evening. They both involve smiling and chatting up those coming to or leaving the mountain. I enjoyed watching the reaction of the locals during those duties. Initially, I thought they wanted to ignore me, but after a while, it became clear they were quite willing to respond positively to a friendly welcome or farewell. When you smile at someone and say something nice like, "Have a great day," or "How's it going?" it's difficult for them to ignore you or say something negative.

The hosts themselves are an interesting group. I may be incorrect with the percentages, but it appears to me about 30% of the hosts are in an age group that would qualify them for AARP membership. The other hosts seem to be in their 20s. I haven't met any of an intermediate age, other than Lee Ann and her assistant, Bruce. It isn't a new experience for me to work with younger people. When I practiced law, I spent a large part of my time working with young associates, frequently serving as a teacher and mentor. But here, it's different. I'm on the same level professionally with the younger folks. If anything, I'm at a bit of a disadvantage, at least to the extent our work depends on physical ability and stamina. Yet, we're all treated as equals and we work together as a team, learning from each other.

I'm also discovering my vocabulary needs some work. *"Like, it's a bummer"* when you're not all communicating on the same level. On the other hand, "*it's sweet*" when you do. I now know how the television character, Monk, felt when he tried to "*get down*" with "*the dudes.*" I know I don't have the current lingo yet, but I'm working on it.

I've also discovered an obvious truth: people treat you differently when you're in a JHMR uniform. For example, if you're free skiing and offer to help someone step into a ski binding on a steep slope after they've lost a ski, they'll likely decline, particularly if it's a young woman. However, if you're in uniform, the skier will almost always accept the offer.

When it comes to dealing with an injured person, I received some advice from Francesca Hammer (the mother of Olympic hopeful, Max Hammer) the other day. When helping someone who may be injured, first get eye contact and have the person take deep breaths. She also said it's more important to get to the injured person quickly, then worry about securing the area. I suspect that's good advice, unless the injury has occurred in an area that is not clearly visible from all directions.

December 22 (Thursday)

Before leaving the mountain yesterday, I was assigned to give a complementary tour this morning. I was looking forward to it, but was concerned that I might not have anyone to give it to. It was overcast and the snow was crusty from a melt that started the day before. I couldn't persuade our house guests (Rick and Remy Weiss) to take advantage of the complementary tour, and a family from out of town we'd met at a restaurant the night before failed to show despite my offer to give them a first class tour. When I couldn't find anyone to join me, and our assistant host leader, Bruce, declined my offer to give the tour to another first time host (Jen Hammer), I was assigned to join Travis Raymond, at the gondola for the day.

When working with another host on a run, you take turns standing by the mountain map at the top of the lift and actually skiing down the mountain. When one of the hosts heads down, he or she often takes a route the other hasn't just completed, or a route taken by skiers who appear to be having difficulty. The idea is to be where the skiers are and to help visitors before a serious problem develops. During our orientation, Lee Ann encouraged each of us to stop from time to time and look around for potential problems—in effect, to be proactive in preventing accidents and mitigating problems that might develop on the mountain.

As I made my runs from the top of the gondola, I noticed that occasionally when I stopped on the slope to look around, another skier would stop nearby and wait for me to continue down the mountain. I became a bit self-conscious, particularly if the other skier had (at least from my perspective) better form than I did. In those cases, I would wait … and wait … and wait, all the time looking around at those on the run, until finally the other skier would take off. Then, I'd follow. That way, the skier couldn't actually evaluate my form—and the reputation of the Jackson Hole Mountain Hosts wouldn't be diminished.

Sick, isn't it? I've got to deal with this issue before too much time passes.

On one of my rides up the gondola, I was with a family of five from New Jersey (two girls, a boy and their parents). The ride takes about seven minutes and

I learned that the mom, Dorothy, hadn't been on skis for two years, they'd never been in Jackson Hole and it was their first run. When she last skied, Dorothy rated herself as a beginning intermediate. She was understandably nervous, particularly since runs off the gondola are generally geared to those who would be considered a competent intermediary, advanced or expert skier or snowboarder. Scott, her husband, showed no sympathy. He kept saying, "Stop whining," until the son finally stepped in and defended his mom.

As a host, I had two—not necessarily conflicting—obligations: to be pleasant (even to Scott) and make everyone comfortable with the mountain and their decision to start on the gondola; and to help poor Dorothy get to terrain that would be more suitable for her first day. It was a challenge, but by the time the gondola deposited us at the top of the lift we were all on the same page, and I was able to send my newly adopted NJ family off on a route I thought Dorothy would be able to handle.

On another of my runs off the gondola, I came across a family of three (a mom, dad and an adorable six-year-old daughter). I encountered them on lower Gros Ventre, an intermediate run, and their daughter was having some difficulty. Finally (and predictably) she fell and lost a ski. The dad was below her by ten yards or so, and the mom, while still up slope, wasn't likely to be much help since she was precariously close to falling herself. I waited for the dad to make his way up to Miss Adorable, but instead he simply shouted at the poor child in an abusive manner.

In my judgment, based on life experience and not mountain hosting instructions, the last thing a host should do is to interfere with the interaction between parent and child. On the other hand, I couldn't just stand there like a tree stump in the middle of the slope and do nothing. So, I slid down and positioned my skis just below the child's to give her a platform to do what her father was demanding of her in an irritating tone. I didn't say anything and simply waited for him to make his reluctant way up to the two of us. By the time he arrived, his daughter was back in her bindings and was ready to resume skiing. I smiled, told them to have a nice day, and watched as they made their way down the slope. While they were still within ear shot, I heard the young girl say, "I never want to take that run again."

The day was coming to a close at the top of the gondola and visibility was diminishing rapidly. I was standing near the map board when I saw a skier coming my way with one ski on and the other under his arm. He was with his teenage daughter, a snowboarder, waiting for him at the top of the GV run. He couldn't get the ski on.

At a glance, it was evident he'd failed to cock the binding and had too much snow caked on the bottom of his ski boot. Recalling my recent experience at the host try-outs in attempting, unsuccessfully, to fit my own boots into the bindings, I sympathized. I helped him with his other ski, and since it was late in the day and nearing white-out conditions, I directed them down Lupine Way and suggested the Nez Perce Traverse over to Casper. I waited awhile, then took the very route I'd suggested.

I found him struggling on the road headed to Amphitheater. As I passed him, I looked over my shoulder and said, "Follow me"—then I lost my balance and fell. By the time I caught up with them again, they weren't far from the Nez Perce Traverse and, as I committed to it, I heard the daughter say, "But dad, I can't do a traverse on my board." Too late; I was gone and was in no position to return and help him find an alternate route down the mountain. I'd just failed my hosting duties.

A while later, on my way over to Casper, I felt a little better after encountering several confused skiers and leading them down to the South Pass Traverse and on to the bottom of the mountain.

December 23 (Friday)

I worked today, substituting for Lynnie. She'd worked for me on the prior Tuesday while I attended Ski & Race Camp. I was assigned with Matt Lamb to Thunder in the morning and Après Vous in the afternoon with sweep duties on AV. The host with sweep duties has to check in with the Ski Patrol at the top of AV at 3:45 p.m. If a number of the patrollers are out on the slopes picking up bodies, they'll use a Mountain Host to fill in. The sweep off each lift begins fifteen minutes or so after the final load of skiers and snowboarders has been deposited at the top of the run.

In each Ski Patrol shack there is a package of laminated instructions on the precise routes to be taken by those assigned to sweep duty. The mountain appears to be divided into corroders, each of which looks to be about two hundred yards wide, depending on the nature of the terrain.* The corroders run from the top of the ski area to the bottom. The person assigned to sweep a corroder traverses back and forth, in and out of trees, looking for people who haven't made it down the mountain. As you're descending, the instructions specify where you are to stop from time to time and wait until the person in the next corridor has reached his or her designated stopping spot and is able to give an all clear signal.

---

*   *This is a guess and, if accurate, would result in about forty or so corroders if you assume each has an average length of under 4,000 vertical feet on a four square mile surface. And there appear to be about forty ski patrollers working at the mountain on any given day.*

That process is repeated until the entire in-bound ski area has been covered.

The morning was uneventful, at least until about 11:00 a.m. I was at the top of Thunder, giving directions to folks wanting the easiest way down when my boss Lee Ann arrived. As I started talking with her, Bill Iams (a member of my Race Camp group) and one of his skiing buddies came by and tried to persuade me to take off with them and have some fun. When he learned who Lee Ann was, the two of them left us. I assured Lee Ann I wasn't in the habit of taking off with friends while on duty.

About forty-five minutes later I was making my way over to the Casper mid-mountain restaurant to meet up with our house guests for lunch, when I spotted the Mountain Imaging photographer in the middle of the Casper run. No one was around, so I signaled that I wanted my picture taken, thinking it would be nice to have a photo in my uniform. I sped down the run toward him, trying (with minimal success) to use all the techniques I'd picked up during my six days of Ski & Race Camp, and came to a halt in a swirl of snow just below him—and, as it turns out, next to Lee Ann!

What could I say? Busted on my fourth day of work.

Lee Ann is a telemark skier and is always on the move. She seems to have eyes in the back of her head and can appear at any time, without warning. I have the impression she'll know if you aren't doing your job.

I wanted to redeem myself this afternoon, so I made it a point to be at the top of AV at precisely 1:00 p.m. and to keep to my rotation. The afternoon passed without incident, but the wind started gusting, the temperature dropped and the snow became crusty about midway up the mountain. I kept taking runs to avoid freezing and waited for the day to come to an end. It got so cold around 3:00 p.m. that I spent five or ten minutes with the lift operator in the glassed-in booth at the top of the run and, luckily, wasn't spotted by Lee Ann. At about 3:30 p.m. I went into the Ski Patrol shack, ostensibly to wait around for sweep duties, despite knowing it was unlikely I'd be needed since there'd been no serious mishaps at AV that afternoon.

I asked the lead patroller in the shack, Kevin, what run I would be asked to handle if I were needed for sweep. and his response was, "An easy run—St. Johns". That got my attention since an easy run in my view would be down the center of AV, not St. Johns, a double blue run which is rarely groomed and one I have yet to take this year. I've made a note to check it out before I'm actually called upon to run a sweep from the top of AV under difficult conditions.

December 27 (Tuesday)

I started the day at the top of the gondola as "barn boy" with Trevor Robinson. The barn at the top of the gondola houses a limited number of ski lockers and a pizza stand.[*] Those with lockers in the barn, and ski instructors with students, are allowed to ride to the top before the general public is permitted to do

---

[*] *Several years later the ski lockers and pizza stand were removed from the barn.*

so. The barn boy has to hold all those early arrivals in the barn until the mountain is officially opened, usually at 9:00 a.m., unless there's been heavy snow and the Ski Patrol is working to protect skiers against avalanches. It's precisely on those powder days that it's most difficult to hold the anxious skiers in the barn. Everyone wants to make first tracks down the mountain.

We had about nine inches of fresh, fluffy powder this morning. I took the first run down Gros Ventre and have to admit to conflicting emotions. I was really nervous because I'd rarely skied in powder. Actually, that's an overstatement. I'd **never** *skied* in powder. I just pointed my skis downhill and struggled to stay upright with limited success. Learning to actually *ski* in powder was going to take some time. However, I did manage to make several creditable turns and got an inkling of what it actually feels like to float through light powder that covers the tops of your boots. It can be exhilarating.

After my first run down GV, Lee Ann decided I was needed elsewhere. I was first asked to be a back-up tour host. I met Ben, Hallie and Austin from Cincinnati, but the primary host got the tour. I was then sent to Après Vous to join Scott Spitzer and Travis Raymond. It was a busy morning on the beginners run below AV, and the three of us were asked to take turns at the top of the Teewinot lift picking up bodies (I called it "tossing tots").

On crowded days, it's not uncommon to have crashes at the top of the beginner lift as people drop off the chair. Part of the problem is caused by ski instructors who fail to move their charges out of the way quick enough after off-loading. A Mountain Host is often assigned to help clear away the human debris before the next chair unloads and adds to the pile of bodies, skis and snowboards. The other problem is frequently caused by snowboarders who stop in the middle of the ramp to fit their free foot in the bindings, blocking the way for those on the next chair.

I've concluded I don't have a great deal of sympathy for snowboarders and I'm going to have to go through an attitude adjustment if I expect to make a good Mountain Host.

My generally negative feelings about snowboarders were reinforced later in the afternoon at the top of AV. I'd skied down a slight incline and stopped next to the restroom when a young fellow on a snowboard slammed into me from the rear. When I said, "What the hell do you think you're doing?" his response was, "Dude, you stopped." He then took off as I struggled to pick myself up.

This afternoon, I was assigned to Thunder and had Aloha duty at the end of the day.

December 29 (Thursday)

We had another epic day with continuing snow and high winds. The tram and Sublette never opened due to avalanche danger and high winds, and Thunder didn't open until about 2:00 p.m. I was assigned to AV in the morning with Dave Hopper and Matt Lamb. I couldn't quite work up enough nerve to ski St. Johns because it hadn't been groomed and there was a lot of fresh powder on top of moguls—or so I imagined. Instead, I stayed on the more modest runs at AV, skiing in powder on top of groomed terrain. I was trying to get used to it, but it was slow going.

The snow in Jackson and at the mountain is the most we've had since 1997. There's at least several inches of new powder each morning and the snow depth has been sufficient to allow the resort to open all runs, even those like Saratoga which I'm told is often closed early in the season because of exposed rocks. I've decided that if I'm really going to become a legitimate Mountain Host (instead of going through the motions and pretending), I've got to learn how to ski in powder conditions and handle difficult terrain off the groomed runs.

I was moved to the gondola at the beginning of the afternoon because Thunder was still closed. Around 1:30 p.m. I got word Thunder would open half an hour later and was asked to help control the lines at the bottom of the lift. Everyone on the mountain had heard it was about to open, and since the tram and Sublette were still closed, the only way to access much of the south side of the mountain would be to take the Thunder Quad Chair.

When the maze at the bottom of a lift grows to a point that the lines extend out beyond the ropes, hosts are asked to assist in controlling the lines and ensuring an orderly merging of groups to give all an equal opportunity to access the lift. There's a separate line reserved for staff and instructors with students. The idea is to allow three to four groups of the public skiers and snowboarders through for every one group of instructors, students and staff. The locals and staff understand the process and help keep the uninitiated under control.

However, with all the untouched powder on the slopes, there was considerable pressure to move through the line as quickly as possible. When the first chair was loaded by the initial four skiers and snowboarders in line, everyone burst into applause. And when the first of those same people arrived back at the bottom of the lift, at skiers left of Riverton Bowl, there was more applause.

I spent what remained of the afternoon at Thunder with Dave and Matt. As a host, we get more runs than the general public, even if we spend ten minutes or so at the top of the lift answering questions in front of the map board, because we're able to go through the staff line with a minimal wait time. The objective, of course, is to keep the hosts on the mountain where they are most likely to encounter problems or those in need of assistance. I was still struggling with the powder and, given the depth of the new snow, tried to take the easiest way down each time I was expected to take a run.

The first time down I stayed on Amphitheater, the only single blue run to the bottom of the lift. Near the top of the run, I skied into a snow drift and was almost buried. About 95% of those taking the Thunder lift were advanced to expert skiers and all were taking the double blue and black runs to the bottom, while I struggled through virtually untracked powder on the single blue run. By late afternoon, I was frustrated and nearing exhaustion.

That's when Dave suggested we take a run together and "find something hard." When I begged off saying I was tired, his response was, "Hey, old man, your legs can't be tired yet." Little did he know.

On one of my last runs down Amphitheater this afternoon I ran across two young fellows, one on a snowboard attempting to help his buddy put back on an errant ski. I tried to help, but we couldn't seem to fit the boot into the binding. I called Bruce for advice. He said once I'd determined for sure that the binding was broken, I could call the Ski Patrol and ask them to bring a spare ski. He cautioned, however, that I not call the patrol "until you've verified that there's a real problem." I got the message and took a more careful look at the kid's ski. I figured out how to adjust the binding, helped him fit his boot into it, and sent them on their way. Another lesson learned.

I was actually glad to make my way to the bottom this afternoon and to go to Aloha. I've concluded that I still have a long, long way to go before I'm really capable of doing my job on powder days and on the more difficult terrain that actually accounts for more than 70% of the four square miles of terrain at JHMR.

December 30 (Friday)

I substituted for Lynnie again today. I was assigned to the gondola in the morning with Dede Burnstine and Matt Lamb. We had a good rotation.

In the early afternoon, I had speed control which involves moving from spot to spot on certain assigned runs where speeders are known to be. You attach a brightly colored flag to the end of one of your ski poles and when you see a speeder approaching, you raise the pole. Your presence is supposed to give the speeder pause and, hopefully, cause the speeder to slow down. The area where speeding is most likely to occur is often at an intersection of an advanced and an intermediate run. Amphitheater is a notorious area for lower level intermediate skiers and snowboarders coming down Lupine Way to encounter advanced or expert skiers coming off the Cirque, Paint Brush or the Thunder run (often called 'tourist trap' by the locals because it looks easier than it skis). More often than not, speeders are young teenagers, both snowboarders and skiers. They're generally respectful, but not always.

Late in the afternoon, I helped a family from Ireland (Kate, Matt and Mark) on lower Sundance Gully. Mark was about ten-years-old and had become frightened. His fear was palpable and he refused to move. In cases like that we could call Ski Patrol and ask for a courtesy sled to the bottom of the mountain. But before making that request we are first expected to try to solve the problem. I did so, and was able to persuade Mark, with me beside him, to side-slip down the entire way to the gate leading to Eagle's Rest, one of the beginner runs. It was tedious and took a long time, but we made it to the bottom without having to burden the Ski Patrol.

Each host has been provided with an annotated map of the mountain listing the names of various locations. Most of the names aren't shown on the Mountain Map Guide made available to the public. When a Mountain Host comes across a person in need of a sled, whether they are injured or need a courtesy ride, the host is supposed to radio Mountain Station, giving the nature of the problem and a precise description of the location. It's critical that the location provided is accurate. Sleds are positioned at various locations and elevations around the mountain, and the responding ski patroller will bring a sled positioned close to where it may be needed. The last thing we want is the sled arriving below the intended site, particularly if there's an injury involved.

January 3, 2006 (Tuesday)

It snowed all night and there was a lot of new powder. When I went into the Mountain Host office to pick up my radio, Lee Ann was there. She said I was lucky—I had been assigned to Tram 1 duty.

Today was the heaviest powder day of the year, with about two feet of fresh snow at the top of the mountain, and the gondola was closed. The closure was caused by a tree that had been blown over and hit one of the cars. It would be several hours before they could get it back into operation. That meant the only effective way to access the terrain on the south side of the mountain would be the tram. Anyone assigned to it would have the best powder skiing of the year.

Dave Hopper was in the office at the same time picking up his radio and, to his astonishment, I told Lee Ann I was uncomfortable taking Tram 1 today.

Tram 1 duties require the host to ski from the "Top of the World" to the bottom of the mountain seven times during the day. The last run could involve sweep duty in the Hobacks, a series of black diamond runs I've never had any intention of taking. Thankfully, Lee Ann said there would be no problem finding someone else to take Tram 1 duties (Dave was salivating at the possibility), and I was reassigned to tour duty in the morning and Casper-Sweetwater in the afternoon (the advanced beginner area).

As it turned out, the tram didn't open until after 9:30 a.m. due to avalanche concerns. It was a zoo at the bottom of the mountain, with people hiking up to the Sweetwater lift to get up to Casper and the upper mountain slopes.

I was actually able to assemble a group of people interested in taking a mountain tour. They included Norm and Gail, an older couple from Toronto, and Jay and Tracey, a young couple from Colorado Springs. We made it as far as Thunder. They were as uncomfortable as I was with the powder, particularly when we ran into a snow drift on the upper Amphitheater run. By then it was approaching noon and we headed back to the Casper restaurant along the Nez Perce Traverse. So far as I could tell, we were the only skiers on the mountain heading north and had to break a trail through the powder on the relatively flat traverse.

As the leader, I was the one breaking trail, and at one point when I was out of breath I stopped and told the group about visiting Yellowstone the prior winter and watching a herd of bison walking single file through deep snow. As the lead bison tired of the effort, it would step aside and the next in line would take over the task. The young fellow from Colorado Springs got the point and took over as lead "bison" for the next fifty yards or so. It was rough going but we made it back to the Casper restaurant.

The group invited me to join them for lunch, and I accepted. What I really wanted was a dollar tip so I could frame it. However, I had made the mistake of mentioning that Barbara and I have an apartment in

Paris. After hearing that, the chance of receiving a tip (something I was anxious to receive for the first time in my life) was non-existent.

The afternoon at Casper was generally uneventful. I practiced some powder runs but stayed on the easy terrain that had been groomed before the heavy snow.

January 5 (Thursday)

I was assigned to Après Vous in the morning and Thunder in the afternoon. There was a serious inversion layer with zero degrees at the base of the lift and temperature in the mid-teens at the top. I encountered a skier with his skis off, sliding down lower Warner (a double blue run) on his butt. Apparently, he'd determined the slope was too steep for him and the safest way down was in a sitting position. There were lots of beginner-type and low intermediate skiers on AV because it was heavily groomed and it was a bright clear day. I guess they'd decided it looked easy enough from the bottom of the lift to give it a try.

For the most part the day was uneventful, except for one moment when I was on route from AV to Thunder. At the top of the gondola, as I was exiting the lift, I slipped on an ice patch and fell flat on my back right in front of Bruce. I'm badly bruised and will be sore for several days.

January 6 (Friday)

I substituted for Julian Gee who was traveling in Europe, and was assigned once again to Après Vous in the morning and Thunder in the afternoon. AV was much like it had been on Thursday, heavily groomed with an inversion layer. Today was a clear sunny day with lots of beginner-type skiers on the run. I had an easy rotation with Rory ("Hollywood") who was just back from Pasadena and the USC-Texas national championship football game. Almost every time I arrived back at the map board at the top of the lift, I found one or more attractive young women consulting him about the best route down from AV—as if there was really much of a choice!

In the afternoon I was paired with Matt Lamb at Thunder. It turned out to be another uneventful day, helping people who had fallen put back on their skis. I mentioned to Matt that my boots felt a little like bedroom slippers. He said it would make a big difference if the boots were a tight fit and I should consider getting new linings.

There were few people on the slopes late in the afternoon, and Lee Ann released me early. I decided to follow Matt's advice and stopped by the Bridger Center sports shop to arrange getting new, fitted linings put in my boots. I believe it could be important because, as I was leaving for the day, Bruce asked if I was ready to take on tram duty next week. I told him I was, while silently hoping it would not be on a powder day. We'll see how it goes.

January 10 (Tuesday)

I was assigned to Casper and Sweetwater in the morning, the gondola in the afternoon and Aloha at 3:30 p.m.

The morning was generally uneventful. I met a fellow named George Ingle (a former Lockheed executive and member of the Board of the Conservation Alliance in Jackson) on the Casper chairlift, skied a run with him and had lunch with him at the Casper restaurant. George is in his early 70s.

The afternoon was spent skiing off the gondola. I felt lethargic and skied with a great deal of hesitancy, despite the fact that I now had new, tight fitting boot liners. I was glad when the time came to head down to Aloha duty. I've staked out a spot for Aloha duty next to the Mountain Imaging Building. It's located about thirty yards or so above the base area where most of the other Mountain Hosts congregate. I get first crack at the departing skiers and snowboarders and seem to elicit more positive responses from them than I do when I stay at the base area. I enjoy the brief exchanges and I'm able to avoid walking down and, more importantly, up the extra distance.

January 12 (Thursday)

Paul Turi and I were assigned to the gondola the entire day and to Aloha duty at 3:30 p.m. We had barn-boy duty and one of us would get to take the first run down the mountain and radio in the gondola report. There was about eight inches of powder overnight, and I offered the first run to Paul. Before the public began arriving at the top, I went into the demo tent located at the top of the gondola and checked out a pair of wide powder skis.

This was my first time using powder skis and I immediately felt more comfortable when I took my first run down the mountain. I had much more control and thoroughly enjoyed the trip down Gros Ventre. The second time I was preparing to take a run on the powder skis, a young bellman from Spring Creek Ranch named Chris Wheeler stopped by the map board. Chris was a former member of the U.S. men's development ski team. He suggested we take the run together, so we headed down GV.

I did my best to keep Chris in sight as we sped down the slope. That young fellow made it look so easy, and I worked so hard. When he turned, his uphill knee came within an inch of the snow. But I found I was skiing with a great deal more confidence and no longer felt confined to the groomed areas. At the base, I thanked Chris for the run. As I headed to the staff line, Chris said, "Thank you, Mr. Adams."

Back at the top of the gondola, I mentioned to Paul that I enjoyed skiing on the powder skis but found them a bit difficult to handle on the hard pack at the base of the mountain. Paul suggested I try the K2 Apache Chief skis. I went back to the demo tent and exchanged the wider powder skis for the K2s. On my next run I found those skis even more liberating than the other pair. I ended up taking about four or five runs on the K2s before switching back to my all-terrain Atomic skis. I had made a breakthrough, and for the first time I felt some comfort skiing in powder.

Also for the first time I was beginning to believe that if faced with the need to reach an injured skier half buried in powder on ungroomed terrain, I'd be able to do so.

On one of my last runs on the K2s I spotted a young mother, Shannon, with two children on GV. One was an eight-year-old girl, Blair, and the other a five-year-old boy named Camden. Camden didn't have poles and, like so many young kids, would ski in a perpetual snow plow, weaving back and forth across the run. Occasionally, Camden would do the splits and end up in a face plant. The little kids have a center of gravity so low, and they are so flexible, they can roll around in the snow and bounce back up with no discernable effort.

GV had become pretty chewed up during the day, and Camden was skiing over moguls almost half his size. Blair would ski ahead, followed by Camden, and their mom would bring up the rear often standing and watching as Camden would fall, sprawled in the snow, untangle himself, and somehow stand up, often with skis crossed (and at times, pointed in opposite directions). As I watched the scene unfold, one of Camden's skis popped off, and he was having some difficulty putting it on. His mom didn't make a move to help, so I skied over to give him a hand. His helmet was caked with snow, and he could barely see out of his goggles. He thanked me as he skied off in his snow plow.

I went on and stopped further down the run in front of a stand of trees. The route to skier's right of the trees was the easiest way to the bottom and to skier's left was a fairly difficult double blue run named Slalom that is rarely groomed and was considerably chewed up. As I watched Shannon and her two children approach the cross roads, Camden pointed his skis downhill and zoomed past me to the left, heading toward Slalom. By the time Shannon reached me, Camden had gone beyond the point of no return and was committed to the Slalom run. Fortunately, he fell before heading into the trees on the right side of the run. I was concerned he would head in the wrong direction down an even steeper double blue run named FIS, and suggested to Shannon that they follow me down the Slalom run. We made it to the bottom, and after giving high-fives to Camden and Blair, I left them.

On my next to last run of the day, I came across a snowboarder who'd injured his rotator cuff at Corbet's Couloir. I saw a ski patroller higher up the slope and signaled him. When he arrived, I headed to the bottom.

It was a terrific day on the slopes, and possibly the beginning of a breakthrough for me.

January 13 (Friday)

I bought the K2 Apache Chief skis. Now I'm looking forward to trying them out on powder.

Breakthrough: Host or Ghost

January 15 (Sunday)

I went free skiing today with Lowell and Pam Martindale, two of my former law partners (and co-owners of our Spring Creek Ranch town house that we'd purchased in the early 80s), and with Brent Backman who had been in my Ski & Race Camp group. They took me on two runs I'd never tried. The first was Gannet, the double blue run off the Thunder lift. It wasn't groomed and we got some good, choppy powder. We also took Tensleep, a black traverse to the Cirque off the top of the Sublette lift. The route goes under Corbet's Couloir, down through some trees, and on to the top of the Cirque, a black run. The powder was still good and the skis really performed well.

I've definitely made a significant breakthrough with my skiing.

Bill skiing powder on a free skiing day.

January 17 (Tuesday)

Today I was assigned to give a complementary mountain tour in the morning. I thought I'd hit the jackpot because I had seven takers: John and

Michele from Montreal (John is a corporate lawyer with Stikeman Elliott); Silvan and Doreen, also from Montreal (both of whom are translators and know John and Michele); Steven, a sixty-four-year-old fellow from Connecticut who'd taken a guided tour given by Barb Burris the day before; Shelly, a young mother from Ogden, Utah whose husband is in training for avalanche control; and Lowell Martindale, my former law partner.

Sublette had been closed for a while in the morning and it didn't appear that I'd be able to take the group over to that side of the mountain. However, we did ski Laramie Bowl off the top of the Thunder lift. The second time we took the gondola up, I heard on the radio that they'd opened the Sublette lift and we headed back in that direction. Lowell had to split off at that point.

We skied Egg Carton and Grand to Sublette, and at the top of Sublette, we skied down Rendezvous Trail, then back to Casper for lunch. Before leaving the group, Lowell had blown my chance to receive a tip by disclosing I have an apartment in Paris.

In the afternoon I was alone on Après Vous and had been assigned to check in for sweep duty. If it is a particularly cold or windy day, as it often is in the late afternoon, it's not unusual for the host to take a seat in the Ski Patrol shack and spend ten or fifteen minutes with the patrollers even if the host is not needed to assist in the sweep. And that's exactly what I did.

There were five patrollers in the shack, and as we chatted the conversation turned to deadly accidents that had happened over the past two years. One of the patrollers had been first on the scene last winter to find the remains of a young fellow who'd shot off the edge of a groomed trail near Saratoga Bowl. He apparently had been traveling at a great speed and bounced off several trees, losing most of his scalp. He'd hit a tree with such force, his gloves ended up down slope by about ten yards. According to the patroller, he'd lost a massive amount of blood and the man was pronounced dead at the scene.

They also talked about a lady skier, Heather Donahue, who'd been killed in front of her husband by a sixteen-year-old snowboarder from Florida near the bottom of Laramie Bowl in February 2005. He had been traveling so fast that he broke his board in half when he hit her. His snowboarding buddy had been taking a video of him speeding down the bowl. The sixteen-year-old was able to walk away from the crash and flew back to Florida the next day.*

Finally, they spoke about Brent Newton, the young father of two from nearby Wilson, who had jumped off a cliff above the top of the Thunder lift and landed on a relatively flat surface. He died of collapsed lungs and other internal injuries while being taken down the mountain.

There is no question that the ski resort is steep and challenging, and a real effort is made by staff to make it as safe as possible, but staying safe is a responsibility that ultimately rests with the skiers and snowboarders who use the mountain.

––––––––––––––––––––

* *A year later we learned the teen-age snowboarder was convicted of criminally negligent homicide and was given a jail sentence.*

January 19 (Thursday)

I was assigned to Après Vous in the morning and was partnered with Julian Gee. The commercial airline race teams were conducting ski races on the Race Course at AV. They'd been in town for the past four days. Apparently, every month during the ski season the group goes to a different resort. Each airlines group has its own parka, and they're quite serious. While I was at the map board at the top of AV giving directions to a couple racers, I turned and saw Barbara. I decided to shirk my host duties for a while, and we took a couple runs down AV together.

In the afternoon I was assigned to the Thunder lift with Julian and Sean Wilson. I've been feeling more and more comfortable with my new K2s and, to the extent possible, was avoiding those groomed runs that I've confined myself to for the past twenty or so years.

About mid-afternoon Barbara's ski instructor, Susan Hedden, stopped to say hello while I was at the map board at the top of the Thunder lift. Susan has been an instructor at the mountain for twenty-six years and works nearby as a wrangler in the summer. She's an excellent skier. She suggested we take a run together and I jumped at the chance. When she asked what run I'd like to take, I recklessly said she could choose. Susan did, and we headed over the Egg Carton and down Gannet, the ungroomed double blue run.

About a third of the way down Gannet, Susan stopped and asked if I'd seen the "Jaws Sign." When I admitted I hadn't, she swung to her left toward Riverton Bowl, a black run. Before we got to Riverton, we found the hand-made Jaws Sign that ominously reads, "You are about to enter Jaws – this is your last chance to turn around." Susan, of course, didn't, so we were committed.

Jaws consists of a couple short but steep and narrow chutes between large boulders requiring rapid, tight turns. We made it without incident, and when we reached the bottom of the Thunder lift, I thanked Susan for the run and headed back up.

It's clear I'm making steady progress, since I wouldn't have been comfortable skiing that run with Susan a week or two earlier. It was Chris Wheeler (the young former ski racer who works at Spring Creek Ranch) who told me that, to really improve, you must ski out of your comfort zone. I'm now on a mission to do just that.

At about 3:15 p.m. Sean, Julian and I were at the top of Thunder with Bruce, Lee Ann's assistant head host. Bruce was about to head down to the MOB, and I asked him what run he intended to take. Before I'd fully considered the implications of my question, I was following him down the mountain. He headed to skier's right of Tower 3. Then, rather than following the normal route that loops around and enters the Egg Carton about mid slope, he sailed straight over the top, negotiated a bunch of large moguls, cut to the left in the direction of Gannet, and swung to skier's right through the trees. It's an unmarked area that I think Bruce referred to as "Sheraton Woods". From there we crossed the upper loop of South Pass Traverse and continued down the chopped powder of a run Bruce called "Contemplation."* At the bottom,

---

*   *To this day I'm not entirely clear what route Bruce took down the mountain, nor am I sure about the names he used. I was too preoccupied trying to follow him.*

I thanked Bruce for the run and once again headed up the mountain. This was a terrific day.

January 21 (Saturday)

It was overcast, snowing and windy, and I'd planned to take the day off today but received a call around 8:00 a.m. from our neighbor, Sally Byrne. She and her husband, Jim, planned to cross country ski with other neighbors, Don and Anne Alstead, at the Taggart Lake Trailhead. They invited Barbara and me to join them and, after some hesitation, we agreed to go.

Neither of us has done any cross country skiing this year, and I struggled a lot. In fact, I fell three times and had a devil of a time standing up each time. We spent about an hour and a half on our skis, and I was worn out.

I'm going to have to invest some serious time on this sport if I want to keep up with our neighbors.

We ended our adventure having lunch at Dornan's, accompanied by a pitcher of dark Guinness beer and a bottle of wine.

January 22 (Sunday)

I had a free skiing day with my former law partners, Pam and Lowell. This turned out to be a day to remember. My confidence was high, in large part because of my successful runs several days earlier on Thunder, first with Susan Hedden and then with Bruce. I suggested we ski the Hobacks. Both Pam and Lowell had skied them in the past and were game to go.

We headed up the gondola, then skied over to Thunder via Gros Ventre. At the top of the Thunder lift, we took Laramie Bowl to the Sublette lift, then Rendezvous Trail over to the entrance to the Hobacks, an entrance I'd skied past without thinking about venturing into for more than twenty years. As we started down the trail I knew we couldn't turn around. We were committed to ski about 2,000 vertical feet down to the Union Pass Traverse.

We started down the North Hoback, a rather narrow run between two stands of trees. The moguls were large, and after a hundred yards or so, we cut to skier's right to access the wider, more open and inviting run down the Middle Hoback. The snow was deep and fluffy, although rather chopped up at the top, but glorious nonetheless. For the first time, I knew what people had been talking about when they spoke of their experience skiing the Hobacks. I felt like the mountain had opened up to me, and I was just beginning to discover a bit of what it had to offer.

When we reached the bottom, we decided to take the tram to the top of the mountain and take another run down the Hobacks, but after spending fifteen minutes in the tram line we concluded it would take too long to reach the summit, and by then it would be too late for another run. I had to meet Barbara at the Spring Creek shuttle at 1:00 p.m.

Before ducking out of the line and heading to the gondola, Lee Ann spotted me and informed me I'd received my first written comment from a visitor to the mountain. Someone had written that he had encountered a friendly and helpful Mountain Host who he liked—"despite the fact that the host was a retired lawyer." Although falling short of being an unqualified endorsement, I felt it was not bad for my first comment from a visitor.

On our way up the gondola I suggested that instead of a second run down the Hobacks, we try somewhere else I'd never skied, Moran Woods. Pam and Lowell were game, and after off-loading we headed down Ranger (this was the black run Ken O'Dell had tried to take me down the day I had my try-out). Today it was groomed, but in any event, it no longer appeared to me to be an imposing run.

We then cut over to Croaky Point on our way to the Casper lift. At the top of Casper, we headed north toward Moran Face, past Sleeping Indian and Wide Open, then dropped into the woods. It was another spectacular run. We picked up the Togwotee Pass Traverse back to Casper for one more trip through Moran Woods. At the top of Casper, Pam waited to hook up with Barbara for a final run to the bottom while Lowell and I took our last run down Moran Woods.

This was my best day yet on skis.

There's no question I've improved quite a bit. Ski & Race Camp gave me a jump start and, of course, the number of days I've skied this year has been an important factor. But I also believe the new boot linings, the K2s and skiing out of my comfort zone have made the difference. I now look back at that epic powder day on December 29th when the tram and Sublette were closed and Thunder didn't open until 2:00 p.m., and of course on January 3rd when I turned down the opportunity to take Tram 1 duty in two feet of fresh powder, and think, '*What a waste of two great opportunities.*' I now know the next opportunity I have to ski powder like that, I won't waste my time in Amphitheater.

We ended today by inviting Pam and Lowell over to the house for melted raclette cheese and wine.

January 24 (Tuesday)

I was assigned to Meet & Greet followed by gondola duty in the morning. In the afternoon, I was assigned to speed control with my final stand in lower

Sundance Gully. It was a bright, sunny day with no new snow. The grooming machines had had a field day since the lifts closed the prior evening, and most of the blue and double blue runs were heavily groomed.

The day was uneventful. I used my new K2s in the morning and stayed off the groomed runs for the most part (so much for avoiding Ken O'Dell's trap of searching out untracked powder rather than hosting). Since I would be on groomed trails in the afternoon while on speed control, I switched to my all-mountain Atomic skis at the lunch break.

I've discovered that when on speed control, simply waving a pole with a brightly colored flag on the end doesn't always cause a speeder to slow down, and hosts are encouraged not to be confrontational. If it's an egregious case or particularly dangerous, the Mountain Host is told to follow the speeder to the next lift and, after radioing Ski Patrol, follow the offending person up the lift. The idea is to have a ski patroller meet the speeder as the offender gets off the lift, and when the host arrives the ski patroller and host can talk to the offender.

The consequences for the speeder could be a loss of skiing privileges on the mountain. The difficulty is determining when to make an issue out of it. There's the obvious tension between wanting to let people have fun and taking preventive action before anything bad happens. Fortunately, I have not yet been presented with such a serious choice.

January 25 (Wednesday)

Today was a free skiing day. Again, it was bright and sunny. I'd arranged to meet Pam and Lowell Martindale, Mike Hammer, Ed Liebzeit and Peter Ordway at the bottom of the gondola at 10:00 a.m. Peter brought a house guest, a retired American Airlines pilot. The seven of us skied until about noon, when Peter had to break away for a lunch date.

At one point, I suggested we take Tensleep off the top of the Sublette lift and ski over to the top of the Cirque. We did, and it was awful. The Cirque was iced over with chopped up hunks of snow. It was not a good move. From there, we went over to Casper and skied the

Sleeping Indian and upper Ashley to AV. On our last run before calling it a day, we skied down skier's left side of St. Johns in the trees and finished up with another new run for me, Secret Slope. The snow wasn't great, and neither was I. This was not my best day skiing.

I saw Lee Ann while I was free skiing and she asked me to come in on Friday and work as a back-up tour host in the morning. It seems there's a large group of people with the Young Presidents Organization (YPO) in residence, and they would like to have a tour of the mountain. My older brother, Bob, had been in YPO, and I said I'd be happy to do so. I also thought it could be my best opportunity to finally get a tip to frame.

When I got home, I calculated that I had skied a total of thirty-three days thus far, nineteen free skiing days and fourteen days as a Mountain Host.

January 26 (Thursday)

Again, I was assigned to the gondola in the morning and to speed control in the afternoon, with my last stand to be lower Sundance Gully.

I've concluded the gondola is one of the least interesting assignments because of the limited runs you can take off of it.* I've also decided I would like tram duty, but only for a half day. I'd have a serious problem taking seven tram runs during the course of the day.

I've decided to ask Lee Ann why she doesn't share the wealth by having two tram hosts in the morning and a different two hosts in the afternoon. That way, no one gets overly tired and more hosts are able to ski the south end of the in-bound terrain.

January 27 (Friday)

I showed up for tour duty expecting to meet members of the YPO group, but at the morning host meeting I was told a couple of other ski groups consisting of about forty people had also asked for guided tours. Several of us were asked to meet those

---

* *When I read this journal entry 17 years after it was written I wondered what in the world I was thinking. It says more about my state of mind and skiing ability at the time than about my knowledge of the mountain.*

folks at the base of the mountain and begin the mountain tours around 9:30 a.m. It snowed most of the night and was continuing to snow. The forecast was for intermittent snow showers all day and for the next several days. The mountain had about six inches of fresh powder, but there was thick fog and very poor visibility. The YPO group had paid "big bucks" to get first tracks off Teewinot and Après Vous beginning at 7:45 a.m. and had already headed up the mountain with other Mountain Hosts.

I resigned myself to the fact that it was unlikely I'd be offered a tip and took six of the first ski group participants to show up. I had in my group two couples. The first was Cory and Jeanine. Cory was a strong skier and Jeanine was competent but hesitant. The other couple was Jim and Carrie. Jim was the weakest skier in the group and Carrie had been a ski racer but was quite uncomfortable with moguls and powder. For that matter, the entire group was uncomfortable with powder at the beginning of the tour. The last two in the group were Randy, an intermediate skier, and Stu, who like Cory was a strong skier. All six were with the Sly Fox Ski Club from somewhere in Wisconsin.

We started with the Teewinot lift and from there headed to Après Vous. At the top of AV, the visibility was so bad we could only see ten yards or so down the slope. To make matters worse, the snow had been churned up by the YPO group during the hour or so before we'd gotten to the top of the run. We stayed close to the tree line and stopped frequently. Before each new start, I described the route we were to follow and the nature of the terrain. By the time we reached the South Pass Traverse, most of the members of my group had fallen at least once as they struggled with the unfamiliar powder, the lack of visibility and the challenge of skiing Jackson Hole. Fortunately, by the time we reached the South Pass Traverse at the top of lower Werner, visibility had improved dramatically, as had the group's confidence.

We skied to the bottom and cut over to the Sweetwater lift and headed up to Casper. At the top of the Casper lift I decided to take them through Timberland. Visibility had improved, the run had been groomed before the snowstorm and there was plenty of opportunity to make first tracks. By the time we were back on the main run at Casper, everyone was feeling great.

From Casper, we skied to Lower Sundance Gully and headed to the bottom of the mountain and the gondola. Unfortunately, at the top of the gondola we encountered heavy fog. I decided to lead the group down Gros Ventre to the Amphitheater Traverse and then on to the Thunder lift. Although the group had become more accustomed to choppy powder, it was difficult at the top of GV. On one of the steeper pitches I'd stopped to wait for the others to catch up and was talking with Cory and Stu when Jim slid past us down the hill, head first on his back. Without thinking I shot off directly down the slope, intending to somehow block him before he collided with an immovable object. It was a bad idea. I hit a berm, flew up in the air and came down on my right shoulder, losing my right ski and one of my ski poles. In the meantime, Jim had halted his slide and was righting himself without any real difficulty. What a dumb move on my part.

I got up, put on my ski, and reassembled the group above the Amphitheater Traverse. My shoulder was quite sore and I was concerned I'd done something to it but could still move my arm, so I decided to finish the tour.

We took the Traverse to the Thunder lift and at the top several in the group said that their legs were tired, they were feeling the effects of the altitude and wanted to head over to the Casper restaurant. It was noon, so we skied down to the South Pass Traverse and I dropped them off at the restaurant. They all thanked me for the tour, and Randy (whose last name is Schultz) handed me my first tip—an old, crumpled five dollar bill. Cory started to pull out some money as well, but I stopped him and said, "The tip from Randy is the first I've ever received, and I'm going to frame it. No other tip is necessary."* With that. I skied off toward lower Sundance Gully.

At the bottom of the Gully I radioed Lee Ann, told her my tour was complete and asked what she'd like me to do for the rest of the day. She said I could either call it a day or work Casper-Sweetwater in the afternoon. I told her I'd take a lunch break and work

---

* *It's ironic. I received the tip from a skier with the Sly Fox Ski Club in Wisconsin, not a YPO member. There can be only one "first ever tip" and before I could arrange to have the old, crumpled five dollar bill framed, I misplaced it. But I'll always remember who gave it to me.*

the afternoon, but my shoulder kept bothering me as I was skiing to the MOB and just before I reached the building Barbara called to me from the Teewinot Quad Chair as she passed overhead. I called back that I'd wait for her. By the time she arrived, I'd decided to stop by the clinic in the Cody House and have the doctor on duty look at my shoulder.

The doctor took x-rays. I had a partial tear of the ligaments in my right shoulder. They put me in a sling and told me one of the ski patrollers, Kevin, would give me a snow mobile ride back to the MOB. Kevin was the patroller who I'd first met at the Ski Patrol shack at the top of AV several weeks earlier when I checked in for sweep. Before leaving the clinic, I radioed Lee Ann and asked her to call me on her mobile phone. She did, and I gave her the bad news, not knowing at that point how long I'd be out of action.

Later that afternoon I had an appointment with our Orthopedist, Dr. James Champa, at Saint John's Medical Center, and he confirmed I had a category two tear. As he explained it, there are four categories, one being the slightest and four being the worst, requiring an operation. I'm lucky, and if I keep my arm in a sling for a couple weeks I can apparently go back to skiing. I called Lee Ann again, this time with the relatively good news I may only miss two days next week. That gives me ten days before the next hosting day on a Tuesday (February 7).

February 4 (Saturday)

Ten days rest will not be enough. It's difficult because it's been snowing almost every day and the powder skiing is the best it's been in years. To make matters worse, a house guest arrived the day after my accident and I was not in a position to join her on the slopes during her stay. I now plan to be back on the slopes on Tuesday, February 14th. I spoke with Lee Ann and agreed to find other hosts that would cover for me on the 7th and the 9th. When I called Lynnie to take one of the days, she informed me that one of the fellows from the Sly Fox Ski Club, Stu, had made a point the day after my accident to ask how I was. It was very thoughtful of him.

February 10 (Friday)

It has now been two weeks to the day since my accident. I have movement back in my right arm and shoulder and have decided to ski for a couple hours later today to see how it goes. If all goes well, I plan to resume my hosting duties on Tuesday the 14th.

I was a bit tentative while skiing today, but for the most part felt okay and have decided to go ahead with my hosting next week.

February 12 (Sunday)

I skied again today, this time with more confidence. I went out with a snowboarder, Jim Lewis, the President of First Bank of the Tetons and a good friend. It was his first or second time out this year, so there was no pressure to try any fancy stuff off the groomed runs. At the top of the Thunder lift, we ran into Lee Ann, and I confirmed I'd be back in action on Tuesday. Jim and I made it over to Sublette before calling it a day and meeting our wives at The Peak restaurant in the Four Seasons Hotel for lunch.

February 14 (Tuesday)

I was assigned to tour duty for the morning of my first day back, the same assignment I had when I had my accident. This time things went well. Once again we had several inches of fresh powder and it was a clear, sunny day. My group consisted of a fellow from Detroit named Nick, and a couple named Troy and Monica from an air base in Idaho. Troy is a fighter pilot and his wife is several months pregnant. The group also included a second couple from Seattle; Bill, a retired chemist and his wife, Loreen. Things went well and we made it all the way to Sublette. Before skiing back to the Casper restaurant, Troy and Monica split off from the group. Bill and Loreen invited me to join them for lunch. I did, but declined their offer to pay.

In the afternoon, I was assigned to the gondola and ended the day on Aloha duty. The afternoon passed without incident. However, this was the day each working group at the mountain was to create some sort of snow sculpture. The best idea the hosts could come up with at our morning meeting was to make a hot tub at the top of the gondola. Lee Ann asked for volunteers to dig it out and I begged off on account of my shoulder. A young host named Shelly Barnes did most of the work, and I thought it came out quite well.

That was before I saw what the other groups had done. The crew at the Bridger Center made a giant dragon with candles for eyes. The tram crew created a beautiful replica of the tram. And other groups had sculpted a gorilla at the bottom of the Teewinot lift and the Simpsons at the top of the gondola.

February 15 (Wednesday)

Today I skied with one of our house guests, Marty Glenn. Marty is a judge and former law partner. He and his wife, Andrea, live in New York City and have a place in Vermont. They're used to groomed terrain and we had several inches of fresh powder. I was feeling more confident and headed for several of the less groomed runs with mixed results.

February 16 (Thursday)

I was assigned to Thunder in the morning and Après Vous in the afternoon, with no Aloha duty. As a consequence, I stopped working at about 3:00 p.m. and was able to catch the 3:30 p.m. shuttle back to Spring Creek Ranch.

February 17 (Friday)

It was the last day skiing for our house guests, Marty and Andrea, and Barbara and I took them out for the morning. We all stayed together on the groomed runs. It went well until I took them to Gros Ventre off the gondola. The snow was a bit choppy, and Andrea fell in the same area where I'd had my accident. We stopped early and had lunch at the Alpenhof.

February 19 (Sunday)

It snowed last night, and I decided to go skiing this morning. I went alone and had one of my best days on skis. I headed up Après Vous first, then skied Saratoga Bowl. I'd never ventured there before and had a great time. The pitch is steep, there are lots of trees and boulders, and the moguls are large. It was a great feeling to make it down without a problem, and my confidence soared.

I did so well I decided to spend the rest of the day off the groomed trails and to try runs I'd not taken before. It's hard to explain how much fun it is to discover this mountain after spending almost a quarter of a century staying on the groomed runs.

The second time up AV, I traversed over to the Casper lift and went down through Camp Ground, then straight into the woods to skier's right of the main Casper Run. I stayed on that course until I was near the bottom of Lower Sundance Gulley. I then went to the gondola and headed to the top. I took Ranger (my old nemesis) down to the Solitude

Traverse back to Casper. I ended the day on Wide Open, skiing in and out of the trees before heading back to the MOB.

I stopped in the host office to check on my assignment for Tuesday and was surprised; I'd been given Tram 1 duty in the morning and Casper-Sweetwater in the afternoon. I couldn't have asked for a better assignment, given my growing confidence. Even better, I'll only have to take four tram rides (as opposed to the usual seven) and won't have sweep duty in the evening when my legs would be shot.

February 20 (Monday)

This was a free skiing day and I was asked by one of our neighbors to give a mountain tour to their son and his sister-in-law. They live in Baltimore, Maryland, and aren't used to powder. It snowed last night, and they had a bit of trouble, but we made it as far as Thunder before we had to head to the Casper restaurant and meet Barbara.

February 21 (Tuesday)

This is my first day as a Mountain Host on Tram 1 duty. In my view, Tram 1 has always been the most challenging. I have to admit, however, I'm only doing half of it. My job is to take the first tram to the top, leaving the base at 8:24 a.m., give a condition report to the other hosts, and be available to guide people down from the top on the hour at 9:00 a.m., 10:00 a.m., 11:00 a.m. and noon. That's four tram rides in the morning. Full Tram 1 duties would include three more rides in the afternoon, the last one involving possible sweep duty.

The forecast was cloudy with snow showers and wind of ten to fifteen mph from the SW. They had two to three inches of new snow on the mountain. I decided to drive because I wanted to get to the MOB well before 8:00 a.m. so I'd have time to organize myself and still make it to the tram dock before the 8:24 a.m. departure. I made it with only five minutes to spare. I hadn't yet realized that the first tram was only for ski patrollers, a Mountain Host, and occasionally a ski instructor giving a private or semi-private lesson.

I was the first to arrive at the staff holding pen on the tram dock and didn't have a clue what to do next. Fortunately, a female ski patroller arrived, and when it was time to position ourselves to board the approaching tram, I let her go first. It was my way of avoiding a blunder but was interpreted as a gentlemanly gesture. In fact, she seemed a little startled when I let her go first. I'm not sure what I would have done if it had been a male patroller.

On the way up the mountain I spotted a coyote. At the top of the mountain there was about six feet of visibility. I cleaned the map board and waited hoping no one would ask to be guided down Rendezvous Bowl since I couldn't see where I was going and didn't have a clue which route to take. Just before 9:00 a.m. the first tram load arrived. It occurred to me that these people laid out a lot of money to come up on the first public tram, for the most part with instructors, so they could make first tracks. They weren't the people that needed to be guided down Rendezvous Bowl by a host. So I made an intelligent decision—I followed the last group of ski instructor-guided folks down the bowl. In doing so, I not only found the way down through the clouds, but I learned something on route.

It did involve a bit of faking it.

Every time the instructor stopped and gave instructions to his group, I would stop nearby and pretend to look around to see if anyone was in trouble. That's not entirely accurate. I would, in fact, look for people in trouble (at least those in more trouble than me). The real problem would be if I actually saw someone. There's no question I'd try to help; I was just not sure whether I'd end up being the helper or the helpee. In any event, I made it down Rendezvous Bowl and started down Rendezvous Trail, but stopped at Bivouac, a black run that had been groomed the day before. We had visibility below the bowl, and when I saw there was only one set of tracks on fresh powder, I took off. It was glorious. I thought, '*How good can it get.*' Nothing beats having almost first tracks in fresh powder on steep terrain. I was one happy old dude.

As I got off the second tram, I met a fellow named Mike. He was a telemark skier from Napa Valley who wanted to be guided down the bowl. I obliged, but I did a terrible job. He fell twice, and I didn't help since I was more concerned about making it myself. I left him at the top of Rendezvous Trail (after skiing past Bivouac), and he said, "Is this the end of the tour?" I said, "Yes," and took off, worried I'd be late for the tram that would get me back to the top of the mountain at 11 o'clock.

As I thought about it, I was a bit embarrassed. I should have spent more time with Mike, and at least made an effort to help him. If I ever have an opportunity to meet Mike again, I'll apologize for doing a lousy job and treating him so poorly.

The third time up the tram, I felt like an old hand. My first ski instructor from Ski & Race Camp, Renny Burke, was taking up a family from New Jersey. When we got to the top, I was approached by two ladies in their late 60s—Suki and Lorinda. They'd been at the mountain many years before but wanted to be guided down. Renny and his students had stopped in Corbet's Cabin for a hot chocolate, and I wanted to take my two ladies down the bowl before they exited the cabin.

I didn't want Renny to see me possibly struggling on the way down.

Lorinda had trouble with her binding, but I stayed with them, constantly casting furtive glances at Corbet's Cabin, hoping Renny and his charges wouldn't emerge. Finally, Lorinda got her skis on and we took off. We made it down the bowl (with only several mishaps by Suki) and headed for Rendezvous Trail. They both declined to take Bivouac, and I parted company midway through Rendezvous Trail and headed back for my 4th and last tram ride of the day.

No one needed my services this time. In part, I suspect, because the sun had begun to emerge and you could see more than fifty feet in front of you. I had my best run down the bowl and was so excited that I missed my traverse over to upper Thunder and on to the Casper restaurant. So I skied down to the Sublette lift and took it to the top. From there, I skied the Laramie Traverse to the top of Thunder, down to Nez Perce Traverse, then to the Casper restaurant.

I had made it through my first Tram 1 duty! It was another great day.

I had lunch with fellow hosts, Sally Berman, who was recovering from a separated shoulder, and her husband, Joel, who had been in my Ski & Race Camp group. I took two runs down Wide Open (a double blue that had not been groomed) and two runs down Moran Woods. I was skiing powder on steep terrain and was loving it. I can now, for the first time, understand Ken O'Dell's comment on our try-out day that the best skiers don't necessarily make the best hosts. And I now understand why a host may be more interested in skiing than hosting. Although I know I'll never make it to that "best skier" category, I will nonetheless have to consciously avoid falling into the trap Ken so accurately described.

February 28 (Tuesday)

I'm back in Jackson after four days in Tucson and two in Newport Beach. I had Après Vous in the morning and Thunder in the afternoon. I was also to be released early (no Aloha duty). Problem was, it was raining below the Casper restaurant and snowing above. I was soaked following Meet & Greet and more so by the time I made it to the top of the AV lift. It continued raining all morning. Whenever you skied below Togwotee Pass Traverse, your skis began to stick like Elmer's glue.

About 11:00 a.m., Lee Ann announced over the radio that all hosts were invited to the Alpenhof for lunch. I changed gloves and my parka on the way, and following lunch, we were all released from duty. There was almost no one on the mountain, and they were sending the tram up the mountain mostly empty.

March 1 (Wednesday)

Today I free-skied with Mike Marshall. He's a sixty-three-year-old hotshot skier in great shape and is an alternate in the "Old Dogs" ski group. Mike participated in Ski & Race Camp, and his time through the gates beat mine by about six seconds. We took the gondola up and skied over to the Thunder lift. From there, we took Grand to Sublette and on to the Hobacks. On route, I discovered how Barbara feels when she's skiing with much faster skiers. They wait for you, and the moment you catch up, they take off. If you try to keep pace, you can lose it completely.

The Hobacks skied surprisingly well, but only because the mountain had five inches of fresh powder after the rain on Tuesday. The tram line was too long, so we took the gondola up once again, then skied Ranger and on over to the Casper restaurant for a welcome break and a bite to eat. I ended my day of non-stop skiing with Mike with a run through Moran Woods. Although I really enjoyed spending time with him, he is not a perfect skiing partner for me. His interest seems to be racing down the mountain, while I prefer taking a moment to stop and enjoy the view or simply take a breather.

March 2 (Thursday)

My assignment today was Thunder in the morning and Après Vous in the afternoon with sweep duty at AV. The morning was uneventful. I saw Susan Hedden while controlling the Thunder lift line and made runs down Grand, Laramie Bowl and Amphitheater.

In the afternoon, I had a lengthy talk with an eighty-three-year-old skier who lives part time in the Aspens. His name is H. Snowcroft. My new goal is to be a Mountain Host when I'm eighty-three.*

Barbara and I will be heading to Newport Beach tomorrow to host an Oscar Party for the 15th consecutive year. We'll return to Jackson on Monday so I can host on Tuesday.

March 7 (Tuesday)

It snowed four to five inches on the mountain last night, and when I arrived at the MOB I learned I was assigned to Tram 1 in the morning. I rushed to make the first tram so I'd be ready at the top of the mountain when the first load of skiers arrived at 9:00 a.m. The wind was howling at level two and visibility was really bad. I prayed no one would ask to be guided down on the 9 o'clock run. Fortunately (for them and

---

*   *It turned out to be an unrealistic goal. Health issues got in the way of it being achieved, but now at the age of 84 I haven't given up the idea of skiing if I can just figure out how to get back into my ski boots.*

me), no one did, and I slowly made my way down Rendezvous Bowl by myself. Since I was going to have to take four tram rides in the morning, I decided to save my legs and took Rendezvous Trail to the bottom of the Sublette lift and South Pass Traverse to lower GV and the Slalom run. There was two to four inches of powder all the way to the bottom, and I loved the run.

At 10:00 a.m. the wind was still at level two and visibility hadn't improved much. Again, no one asked to be guided down but several asked for directions. This time I took Bivouac, and before reaching the Thunder lift I headed down the Lower Tramline run.

At 11:00 a.m. I was asked by a family of three from Ohio (a mom, dad and their twenty-something son) to guide them down the bowl. Visibility was still bad, but the wind had subsided a bit. I did so successfully, then sent them on to South Hoback. Again, I took Bivouac, then went to the bottom via lower Gros Ventre.

I was free once again for the noon run, and after skiing Rendezvous Bowl I took the Laramie Traverse to the top of Thunder and the Nez Perce Traverse to Croaky Point. When I arrived I spotted a group of skiers on the edge of the main Casper run and went to investigate. Two ski patrollers were putting an injured skier in a sled, and I stood guard above them to warn away downhill skiers. I had lunch at the Casper restaurant before starting my afternoon tour at Casper.

In the afternoon I skied Moran Woods, Wide Open, Campground, Lift Line (to pick up a glove) and Sleeping Indian. I also had an interesting, and somewhat disconcerting, experience riding the Casper chairlift. It has a triple chair* and at the bottom of the lift a ski instructor with too many four-year-old students to fit on the chair lift asked me to ride up with one of the children, a very small girl named Emily who, apparently, had been warned by her parents not to let a stranger touch her. She was so small her bottom seemed to be barely on the seat, and as we were riding to the top of the lift she seemed to be slipping under the safety bar. I reached out to

---

*   *Years later it was changed to a high-speed Quad Chair.*

hold on to her, but she resisted my touch and for the rest of the ride I held my hand just above the collar of her parka, ready to grab it if she slipped below the safety bar. I had a vision of arriving at the top of the lift, holding an empty parka.

Thankfully, I made it through the day without an unfortunate incident and headed to the MOB and Aloha duty.

March 9 (Thursday)

My assignment was to lead tours in the morning and handle speeder duty in the afternoon with the last stop in Sundance Gully at 3:45 p.m.

I had four people on the tour: Paul and his wife Carol Sakai, a delightful couple from Palo Alto, California; a fellow named Tom from Ohio; and Judy from New Hampshire. They were all good skiers. It was a powder day, quite overcast with about four to six inches of fresh snow. However, the wind was blowing so hard they couldn't open the tram or any of the lifts other than the gondola and the two lifts for the beginner runs, Teewinot and Eagle's Rest. We had no choice but to join the mob trying to get on the gondola. My hope was when we reached the top, Casper would be open and we could make our way over to the north side of the mountain, which is the normal starting point for a mountain tour.

When we got off the gondola they still hadn't opened the other lifts, but I decided to head over to Après Vous anyway. We did so via upper Sundance to Croaky Point, then skied the left side of a NASTAR course that had been set up on Casper, Ashley Ridge and South Pass Traverse to lower Warner. On route, we picked up some great, untracked powder since almost everyone else had headed to Thunder or went back to the bottom of the mountain off the gondola runs.

At the bottom of Warner, we veered south to the Sweetwater lift since I'd heard on the radio that it was running. The lift was slow, and the crowd of skiers so large, I suggested we head back to the gondola in hopes the crowd there had diminished. It had, and when we got to the top, they'd opened Thunder.

We made it to the Thunder lift ahead of much of the crowd, and at the top I decided to chance taking Grand over to the Sublette lift. I'd hoped that it would open before we arrived but it wasn't, and after waiting for a moment at the bottom of Sublette I started off on the traverse back to Thunder.

I had only traveled about thirty yards when they announced over the radio that they were opening Sublette. I stopped the group, and we all took our skis off and walked back to the bottom of Sublette. We were the second or third chair to head up the mountain, and at the top we headed in the direction of Rendezvous Trail. The visibility was still quite poor, and on Driscoll Drive I promptly skied into a snow bank and buried one of my skis. Paul and Tom had to help dig me out, and we then headed for Bivouac and the Rendezvous Trail. The skiers in front of us had taken Bivouac, and I suggested we make the first tracks on Rendezvous Trail. We did, and it was great! Everyone was grinning at the end of the run.

When we arrived back at the Sublette lift, Judy decided she'd had enough and said she would wait for us if we wanted to take another run on Sublette. We did, and it was almost as good as the first time, although it was beginning to get chewed up. We finished the tour by heading back to the Casper restaurant. I was invited to join the group for lunch. Paul insisted on buying my meal, then gave me a fifteen-dollar tip—my second! He was so appreciative, I didn't feel I could refuse.

After lunch, I headed off for speeder duty around Thunder, the gondola runs and Casper. It was a good day of skiing in fairly difficult conditions, but with great powder.

March 11 & 12 (Skiing in Sun Valley, Idaho)

We were invited by friends from Utah who also have a place in Sun Valley, Chuck and Ann Maak, to stay with them and ski in Sun Valley over the weekend. We headed out by car on Friday morning and arrived about five and a half hours later. The skiing on Saturday was good, but the visibility was poor and the wind was strong. On Sunday, however, it was bright and clear, the snow was soft and the temperature was mild. It was a wonderful day on the slopes, and it was fun to discover a new mountain. Sun Valley, however, is a lot less challenging and varied than our mountain. I believe I'd lose interest in it if I were to ski there for the number of days I've been skiing in Jackson Hole.

March 14 (Tuesday)

I was assigned to the gondola all day, with check-in for sweep duty at 4:00 p.m. It was a really good day, and it felt like I helped more people today than I've had occasion to help for the entire season. Part of it, of course, is finding people needing assistance, whether it is directing them to the easiest way down the mountain, helping them get back into skis that have come off, or knocking ice and snow from the bottom of their boots so they can step into their bindings. Doing the latter is a little like shoeing a horse, except you're using a plastic scraper to remove packed-on snow and ice.

I took a number of runs down Ranger and spent a fair amount of time in the trees. It was a good workout, and at the end of the day I was tired. I checked the schedule for Thursday and was surprised, and a bit concerned, to learn I'm assigned to Thunder in the morning and Tram 1 in the afternoon with sweep duty from the tram.

I better take a day off and not ski on Wednesday.

Sweep Duty

March 16 (Thursday)

I needed that day off but was disappointed to learn that I had missed one of the best powder days of the year on Wednesday. The snow was still good but apparently not what it had been the day before. I took it fairly easy in the morning, trying to save my legs for the afternoon. I skied two runs with my good friend, former law partner and neighbor, Bob Pisano, and his friend Dick from out of town. The first run was down Ranger to Thunder, and the other was down the Grand to Sublette. I then had lunch alone at The Peak in the Four Seasons.

The host on Tram 1 for the afternoon has to take three trams, getting to the top at 1:30 p.m. and 2:30 p.m. to be available to guide people down the bowl, and at 3:30 p.m. to wait at the top for possible sweep duty. At 3:45 p.m. the host has to check in with the Ski Patrol and see if he or she is needed for sweep. Previously I had to check in for sweep duty several times at the top of Après Vous, and once at the top of the gondola, but was never needed. For some reason, I had a premonition that I'd be needed this time.

The afternoon runs off the tram went well and without incident, and on my last tram ride to the top I was standing next to one of the friendlier patrollers, a woman named Mary. I asked her what the most likely assignment would be if a host was needed for sweep. She said the Headwall. That got my attention since I'd never skied the Headwall and didn't know how to access it from the top of the tram. Once we arrived, I had about twenty minutes before I was supposed to check in with the Ski Patrol, so I went into Corbet's Cabin, pulled out my map of the mountain, and tried to figure out how I'd make it to the Headwall. When it was time to check in I wasn't sure I had found the proper route and concluded that, if assigned to that sweep, I'd have to be honest and let them know I'd more likely end up the sweepee than the sweeper.

Sure enough, when I finally went into the Mountain Station office that's attached to Corbet's Cabin I was told there had been so many crashes I would be needed for sweep. With great hesitation, I asked what my assignment would be and was greatly relieved when they said the Middle Hoback, with a ski patroller on either side of me, Kevin (the young one as opposed to the Kevin that had given me a snowmobile ride from the clinic to the MOB after my accident) and Karin. The head ski patroller asked if I'd ever done a sweep, and I acknowledged that I hadn't. He said I wouldn't have a problem.

Sweep doesn't begin from Mountain Station until the last riders have been deposited on the mountain and have started down. That occurs around 4:10 p.m. so I had close to twenty minutes to sit in the office/lounge/locker/conference room used by the Ski Patrol and think about how I was going to make it down the mountain without embarrassing myself or missing a stranded skier.

I sat down, looked around, smiled whenever someone looked my way, and tried to keep my mouth shut and appear relaxed. At one point I spotted the laminated instructions hanging on the wall that detailed the duties of each sweeper. I found the sheet with instructions for the Middle Hoback and read it with care. I was determined to complete my assignment with flying colors, or at least without screwing up.

There were about fifteen ski patrollers in Mountain Station waiting for the word that all was clear to begin the sweep. One other host had arrived (a bit late) to check in for sweep, but wasn't needed since I'd already been tapped. As the time approached, the patrollers began buckling their boots and putting on their parkas and readying their gear. I'd been told those patrollers handling sweeps of Bivouac Woods, Cheyenne Bowl, Bernie's Bowl and the Hobacks were to first sweep Rendezvous Bowl and meet up at the bottom of the bowl. From there, the Hobacks group of three was to ski to the entrance to the Hobacks and wait there until the Bivouac Woods sweeper emerged from the trees and gave the all-clear. Once that happened, the three of us headed into the Hobacks.

Karin dropped off first into North Hoback, Kevin shot ahead to South Hoback and I was left to head down the middle. The good news was, neither Kevin nor Karin were there to witness the inelegant way I made my way down the mountain.

I'd been told that the sweeper responsible for the Middle Hoback needed to keep traversing back and forth across the ridge line to check for skiers on both edges, north and south. If I spotted any skiers, I was to stop and be sure I didn't ski below them. About a third of the way down, I spotted three skiers emerge from the trees on the south edge of the North Hoback. They were followed by another three skiers, then a couple of singles. Kevin called Karin on the radio and asked if she saw what he saw. She said she had. I held my position and waited to make sure the skiers I'd seen remained below me on the mountain and to be sure there were no other skiers hidden in the trees.

After a while I radioed Kevin and asked him if I should continue to wait. Kevin was already waiting on the Union Pass Traverse below the North Hoback. He told me to continue down the mountain and that he had an idea who they were. He called them the "rat pack."

I had a long way to go and went as fast as I was comfortable with. I pushed a little too hard however, and about thirty yards from the bottom, on a very steep pitch, I fell and popped a ski. I put the ski back on without a problem, then realized I had only one pole. I don't use my straps because of a thumb injury I suffered a number of years ago while skiing. My theory is that I would rather lose a pole in a fall than reinjure my thumb.

As I looked up the hill and spotted my pole about fifteen yards above me, I began to have second thoughts about my decision not to use straps. The pitch was so steep, it was almost impossible to side-step up the ten yards needed before I could use the other pole to snag the one up hill. I was concerned about Kevin and Karin (who had now joined him) waiting for me but didn't want to leave my old, funky poles—although I did consider doing so.

I radioed Kevin and Karin, told them I'd dropped a pole and would be a few minutes retrieving it. Kevin said, "No problem," and I proceeded to struggle up the slope. I finally succeeded in retrieving my pole and joined my two patient patrollers. We skied to the Union Pass Quad chair and while riding, I asked Kevin about the rat pack.

He told me that several years ago a local skier had died going into Corbet's Couloir. His friends created a shrine of sorts in the trees near the top of the North Hoback and, from time to time, would take the last tram to the "Top of the World." From there, they would ski to the shrine, pay their respects to their fallen buddy, then ski to the bottom of the Hobacks. Because they were hidden in the trees, we didn't see them as we made our sweep.

My day was about done, and I'd survived. I only had one last problem. I thought the Gros Ventre trail we were about to take at the end of the Union Pass Quad would take us to the bottom of the Teewinot lift and I'd have to hike up the hill to the MOB, something I didn't want to do at 4:50 p.m. after all the work I'd done that day. But as we neared the intersection of our trail with the GV trail, both Kevin and Karin went into a streamlined-racers stance and shot across the merger point into the trees on the other side. I followed suit as best I could and emerged high enough above the Teewinot lift that I was able to reach the Operations Building with very little poling. What a relief.

Back to Hosting & Free Skiing

March 17 (Friday)

I skied today with Bob Pisano and his friends, Dick and Dan. I arrived at the mountain an hour or so before they did, giving myself time to relax at the MOB, read the paper and take one run before meeting up with the three. I stopped in the Host Office and Lee Ann and Bruce were there. They told me I'd received a letter; it was tacked to the bulletin board. The letter was from Paul and Carol, the couple from Palo Alto who had tipped me fifteen dollars after the mountain tour a week or so ago. My first formal note of thanks.

I met up with Bob and his friends at the bottom of the gondola. None had skied the Hobacks, but they expressed an interest in doing so and I was pleased to take them.

We took the gondola and headed to the Thunder lift via Ranger and a section of upper Gros Ventre. As we were approaching the top of the Thunder lift, we saw several ski patrollers loading a crash victim onto a sled, guarded by several Mountain Hosts, including Lee Ann. We decided to take Laramie Bowl to the Sublette lift and avoid the crash site. From the top of Sublette, we skied to the entrance to the Hobacks. After skiing the Middle Hoback and the lower South Hoback, we took the gondola again, skied down to Croaky Point, then went to the Casper lift. From there, we went on to Moran Woods, then to the race course on Après Vous. At the top of AV, we headed in the direction of St. Johns and veered off to Togwotee Pass Traverse and on to Casper. We ended our afternoon taking a run on Moran Face to the lower race course on AV through the trees to upper Hana, then down Hana to the MOB.

It was truly a wonderful day of skiing with more ungroomed, off trail runs than I think Bob had ever experienced.

March 18 (Saturday)

Barbara and I skied with our contractor, Dick Stewart and his wife Karen. The Stewarts are fourth or fifth generation natives of Jackson, and Dick hadn't skied in twenty years. As we took the Après Vous lift, Dick pointed out Crabtree Rock just to lookers' left (or skiers' right) at the top of Teewinot Gully. He told me the rock was named after the owner of Skinny Skies when he broke both legs jumping off the rock about twenty years ago.

We had an easy, short day on AV and Casper, then went to lunch at the Westside Grill in the Four Seasons.

March 20 (Monday)

We had fresh powder, and I went free skiing for several hours.

March 21 (Tuesday)

I was assigned to AV in the morning and Thunder in the afternoon. The day was uneventful. I had a number of off-trail runs from the Thunder lift (down through the woods to skier's right of Gannet).

At the morning briefing, Lee Ann said we'd have to turn in our uniforms at the end of the season and clear out our lockers. She also told us that we'd be given verbal evaluations.

March 22 (Wednesday)

I agreed to work from noon to 4:00 p.m. at the Jackson Hole Free Skiing Open. It was part of a national series sponsored by Subaru and was held at Casper Bowl, a cliff-studded cirque accessible by hiking up Pepi's Bench or straight up from the top of the gondola. I thought I'd have to ski the Casper Traverse and position myself about half way up Casper Bowl. I've never skied that traverse. It's a black run, and I'm told it's like a roller coaster. The other possible assignment was at the top of the Headwall above Casper Bowl. The easiest way to get there (I'm told) is to take the East Ridge Traverse off the tram or Tensleep off the Sublette lift, across the top of the Cirque to the bottom of Pepi's Bench, then hike up to the Headwall.* I haven't taken any of those routes or runs and was a little apprehensive about where I would be asked to go, but as it turned out I was only needed at the bottom of Casper Bowl on the Amphitheater Traverse.

Near the end of the afternoon, with only four men to complete their runs, a young seventeen-year-old from Snowmass, Colorado named Charlie Gaylord crashed into a cliff face and tumbled unconscious about forty yards or so down the bowl. Ski patrollers reached him within minutes and called for oxygen. He was taken off the mountain by helicopter about forty-five minutes after the crash without regaining

---

*   *When reading this journal entry so many years after it was written, I realized this was the route I had identified as the likely way to reach the Headwall while studying the map in Corbet's Cabin as I waited for my sweep assignment off the tram.*

consciousness and delivered to the Eastern Idaho Regional Medical Center in Idaho Falls.*

The mood changed instantly, and the competition was called off for the remainder of the day. I headed back to the MOB, having taken only two runs the entire afternoon (one from the top of the gondola to the Casper lift and one back to MOB at the end of the day).

March 23 (Thursday)

I was assigned again to Après Vous in the morning and Thunder in the afternoon. It was a bright, sunny day and after I got to the top of AV I got a call from Bruce asking me to join Sean Wilson at the bottom to assist with a tour. There were about nine people wanting to take the tour. Most were members of Black Ski, a club from Maryland and the Washington D.C. area. We took the group to the top of AV, then on to Casper before splitting them into two groups according to skill level. Sean is a much better skier

---

* *It wasn't until quite some time later that I learned the young man survived.*

than I am, so I took the slower skiers, Steve from Chicago and three women from Black Ski, Cynthia, Cassondra and Regina. They were terrific to be with and expressed great appreciation for the tour. Steve split off at the top of Thunder to join his wife for lunch at the Four Season's, and I continued on with the three ladies to Sublette and finally dropped them off at the Casper restaurant just before 1:00 p.m. It was longer than the usual tour, but I enjoyed every moment of it.

This afternoon, I worked at Thunder and ended up on Aloha duty.

March 24 (Friday)

Barbara and I skied today with our niece Dayna and her husband Scott Milne from Denver. We took the 8:30 a.m. shuttle to the Village and returned on the 4:30 p.m. shuttle. Their two children, Garrett at five-years-old and Turner at three, were checked into the Kids' Ranch from 9:30 a.m. to 3:15 p.m. Scott asked me to take him down Rendezvous Bowl, so we stood in the tram line for almost an hour. It was our last run of the day and we got down the mountain around 3:30 p.m.

March 28 (Tuesday)

It was an overcast day, and I was hoping for an easy assignment. When I arrived at the host office, Lee Ann said I had Tram 1 in the morning and Thunder in the afternoon and would be free to leave at 3:00 p.m. since there would be no Aloha the last week of the season. I asked if there was anyone else able to take Tram 1 duty, but when she hesitated, I said, "No problem, I'll take it."

When I arrived at the top of the mountain at about 8:45 a.m., the sky was relatively clear, but a cloud bank was moving our way. I decided not to make the 9 o'clock run to the bottom since all those in the first tram car were with instructors and none needed help getting down the bowl. I did take the 10 o'clock run, however, and by then we had near whiteout conditions in the bowl. I ended up following a ski patroller and two of his friends down the center of the bowl. Once we reached Rendezvous Trail, it cleared up enough to see where we were going but the light was still flat all the way to the bottom.

No one needed help down the bowl at 11:00 a.m., so again I stayed in Corbet's Cabin until my last scheduled run at noon. A number of folks who had taken the tram to the top with the intention of skiing down took one look at the whiteout, thought better of it, and took the next tram back down. Thankfully, I had no one to guide down at noon, so I was able to make my way down the mountain at my own pace. I was thankful to have completed my tram duty without incident, although I wasn't proud of my hosting duties today.

The afternoon at Thunder was a welcome relief. The light was flat, but it seemed like a sunny, clear day compared to the morning.

The end-of-season Mountain Host party was held at the Calico restaurant. They served beer and pizza. Many of the hosts contributed the tips they received during the season to help pay the bill and I added the fifteen-dollar tip I'd received from Paul and Carol several weeks earlier.

End of the
Season

March 30 (Thursday)

This was my last day of hosting for the season and Lee Ann had said I would be given an evaluation sometime during the course of the day.

I was assigned to lead a tour in the morning and Thunder in the afternoon. I got lucky because we had a heavy snowfall last night and there was good powder on the upper levels of the mountain. Four people took the tour: a fellow named Junior from Saskatchewan; a former real estate broker from San Diego staying in the Four Season's named Linda; and a couple from Washington D.C., Craig who works with the FAA and his wife Pat, a former legal assistant with Baker & McKinsey who is now with a third world government-run assistance corporation.

We had fresh powder for much of the tour and clear visibility. There was only one brief moment of concern. It occurred after we reached the top of the Thunder Lift and were heading for Grand. Craig was a strong skier and his wife, Pat, was more inclined to stay on groomed runs. During the early part of the tour, I had pointed out to the couple those runs that would allow Craig to ski off the groomed trail in and out of trees while Pat could stay on the open, groomed area. Grand offered that kind of terrain, and Craig, without saying anything to the rest of the group, decided to ski in the trees to skier's right off Grand. I stopped about a third of the way down the slope, and the others skied up to me—all except Craig.

We waited, but he never showed up, and Pat started to become quite concerned. Finally, I radioed the other hosts, asking if there was anyone near the top of Thunder who could ski down and check the trees for one of our tour group who'd gone missing. Bruce responded, saying that he couldn't believe I'd lost a skier on my last day of hosting for the year.

A bit later we found Craig at the bottom of Sublette. He'd skied through the trees and ended up on lower Laramie. I was able to radio the hosts that the crises had been averted and our missing skier had been found.

We parted company with Linda and Junior at the gate to the Hobacks (Linda gave me a five-dollar tip) and I left Craig and Pat at the bottom of the Sublette Lift. Craig gave me a ten-dollar tip, despite my earlier disclosure that I had been corporate partner with O'Melveny & Myers and had homes in Newport Beach and Paris. It seemed odd to me. Now that I no longer cared about receiving a tip, they were being offered right and left.

I had lunch alone at the Casper restaurant and as I was getting ready to head over to Thunder, Barbara and her friend, Pippa, spotted me and called my name while riding on the Casper chairlift. I waited for them to ski back down to the restaurant and the three of us then took the lift to the top and traversed over to Thunder. As we were making our first run down Amphitheater, Bruce called on the radio. He asked me to come down to the MOB. He didn't have to tell me that he wanted to give me my end-of-season evaluation.

Bruce gave me the completed evaluation form to read and sign. It was good, and I've been recommended as a rehire for next year.

I went back to Thunder to finish out my duties for the season and took runs down Laramie Bowl and the woods between Gannet and Grand. On the way back to the MOB at the end of the afternoon, I skied to Casper, traversed through the trees to Sleeping Indian, and went on to Wide Open before heading down.

It was as good a final day of skiing as I could have hoped for. My skiing ability has improved greatly over the course of these four months (and sixty-four days on skis), as has my confidence in skiing off the groomed runs. There's still a great deal of the mountain I have yet to discover and some runs I'll probably never take, but I'm confident that I can handle myself in most areas I am likely to be needed as a host.

Now all I have to do is recover and work to get in shape for next December.

Employee Free Ski Day

April 3 (Monday)

The mountain was officially closed to the public Sunday evening. That was also the official last tram day of the season, at least for the public.

The day after the ski season officially comes to a close, all employees of JHMR and all season pass holders who logged one hundred or more skiing days during the season are invited to ski from 9:00 a.m. to 2:00 p.m. Only two lifts are operated; the tram and the Thunder lift. I decided to take one run from the top of the mountain before cleaning out my locker and calling an end to the season.

I was the first to arrive at the tram dock at about 8:30 a.m. and was the first to walk on the first tram. I also was the last to walk off the tram. Just before docking at the top of the mountain, the tram operator announced that none of us were allowed to ski north of Gros Ventre.

On the ride up, I noticed one of the riders had a camera pointed out the front window taking a video of the tram ride. It was a clear day with excellent visibility, although there were clouds gathering to the west. The car was about two-thirds full, and I waited to start my descent until everyone else had taken off. I figured I'd have about ten minutes lead time over the next tram, and I wanted the mountain to myself.

As I was preparing to head down Rendezvous Bowl for the last time this season, I saw Corky Ward, the departing head of the Ski Patrol, standing alone outside Mountain Station talking on a cell phone. Visibility was excellent, but the snow in the bowl was firm and my skiing was not the best. I took it slow, in part because I didn't want to risk injuring myself on my final run of the season, but mainly because I wanted to enjoy the moment and the solitude. As I neared the bottom of the bowl, I stopped and looked up. I was all alone except for two skiers on the far north side of the bowl coming down through the trees. The main, open part of the bowl was absolutely deserted. As I made my way to the top of Rendezvous Trail, I passed two other skiers about to head down Bivouac. From that point on, the only person I saw during the rest of my descent was a lift operator at the bottom of the Thunder lift. On my way down I would periodically glance back or stop and look up at runs like Laramie Bowl and Grand off the top of Thunder, Amphitheater and Gros Ventre. There was not a person in sight, although I did see a hawk souring above Amphitheater as I skied past.

I was all alone, and it was a magnificent feeling. My only mistake had been in forgetting to bring a camera.

I ended my run by cutting through the woods near the bottom of Gros Ventre as I'd done several weeks earlier while following the two ski patrollers after sweeping the Hobacks. Had I not learned about that trail, I would have come out near the bottom of the Teewinot lift and had to hike back up the slope to the MOB. As it was, I was able to ski to the building. I was a bit nostalgic, but happy I'd made the effort to take that final run and final tram ride to the "Top of the World."

Epilogue

(The next 9 years)

I can't, in all honesty, say I felt like a capable Mountain Host that first year. But I did learn the skills necessary to become one, and after two or three more years of hosting, I became comfortable in the role. I continued working as a Mountain Host for an additional nine years. Every year my confidence and skiing ability improved, but at no time was the improvement as noticeable to me as it was during my first year of hosting.

During the time I was hosting I underwent a total hip replacement surgery on both hips. The left was done in September 2008 and the right was done in April 2015. Both procedures were performed by Robert S. Gorab, M.D., with the Orthopedic Specialty Institute Medical Group in Orange County, California. I was fortunate in several respects. Dr. Gorab has an outstanding reputation, his procedure involves the anterior approach resulting in a faster recovery and I'd been told he's a strong skier. Even better, he has skied at JHMR and knows the mountain.

Before the first procedure we talked about my work as a Mountain Host and he implanted what he called an athletic joint, slightly larger than the normal joint. I had occasion to test his work in December 2008 while skiing down skiers left of the Cirque. If you're too far to the left you can end up skiing off a one or two foot cut in the uphill side of a trail named Horn's Hole Traverse. That's what I did only four months after my first hip replacement, and as I landed abruptly on the trail my immediate concern was whether I had damaged my new hip. I was relieved to discover that I had not, and to this day I feel fortunate to have had him perform my hip replacement procedures.

Bill with ladies from Orange County, California, taking a break in their mountain tour.

Over the years, I had numerous amusing, memorable and rewarding experiences on the mountain. I stopped maintaining a journal of my experiences after that first year of hosting, and while the memory of details may have faded, or may have been conflated in my mind with other events, I still recall many of those moments and some are quite vivid.

There was the time at the top of the gondola when I watched a grandson with a snowboard trying to help his grandmother step into her ski bindings without success. She apparently had not been skiing for quite some time, was nervous and had put her right foot in her left ski boot and her left foot in the right boot. When glancing at her feet she looked like the Eugene Levy character, Gerry Fleck, showing off his dog in the movie *"Best in Show."* Then there was the time when I was asked by a visitor during a mountain tour, "At what elevation does a deer become an elk?"

On another occasion, while working at AV, I came across a young fellow sitting in the snow severely dehydrated. It was a cold day, but he'd removed his helmet, jacket, and gloves, and appeared to be totally disoriented. On that occasion, I radioed Ski Patrol and requested a courtesy sled ride for the young fellow.

One day, when I was standing at the map board at the top of AV, a Spring Creek Ranch neighbor, Paul Frantz, got off the chair lift and came up to me. After chatting a bit, we decided to take a run together. We headed down Moran and made it as far as Togwotee Pass Traverse. Just as Paul took a right turn toward the Casper lift, I spotted what appeared to be an altercation between two skiers down slope and I headed down to see what the problem was. Two middle-aged men were about to come to blows. Each had a young son, and the two kids had either run into each other or come close to doing so. In any event, the fathers intervened, had words, matters escalated, and when I arrived on the scene they were about to take swings at each other. I stepped in, separated the two and radioed Ski Patrol. I then called Paul on my cell phone to tell him I wouldn't be able to join him at Casper for our hoped-for run.

Another time, there was a young woman from out of town who'd crashed near the top of the Sublette lift. I was the first on the scene and determined she'd injured her shoulder. I called Mountain Station, asked for a sled and followed it part of the way down the mountain as they headed to the clinic. The next day, when I was walking up Cache street toward the Jackson town square, the same young woman with her arm in a sling recognized me, stopped me on the street and thanked me for helping her.

I also recall the time when I had tram duty and skied to the edge of the cliff face above Corbet's Couloir and found a thirty-something year old Austrian fellow with really long, skinny skies standing at the edge, his skis extending out over the Couloir while he contemplated taking the plunge. After standing there awhile, he looked over at me and asked if I wanted to go. I said I didn't and asked him what he was going to do. He told me his girlfriend in Austria had recently skied in Jackson, claimed she'd done Corbet's, and challenged him to do the same. "But," he said, "I don't want to break my bones." He asked what I thought he should do.

I had two recommendations. The first was to ski down the mountain to one of the shops and rent shorter all-purpose skis before taking the plunge. The second, alternative suggestion, was to follow me down the mountain, and when he returned home either tell his girlfriend he'd skied Corbet's or confess he'd chickened out. I waited around a while longer while he contemplated his choices and finally continued down the mountain, figuring if he made the jump I'd probably hear about it on the radio. I never learned what he finally decided to do, and for the rest of the day I took some comfort in the fact that I did not hear on the radio a call for Ski Patrol assistance at the bottom of Corbet's Couloir.

I have a fond memory of a rewarding experience that occurred when I was assigned to the Casper lift. I'd been volunteering as a Mountain Host for about six or seven years and was standing at the top of Wide Open when a family of five skied past me and started down the slope. Included in the group was a grandfather several years younger than me, his son and daughter-in-law and two youngsters. The grandfather was having difficulty negotiating the moguls and the rest of the family appeared to be unaware he was falling behind. I began following, staying ten or so yards behind him until he fell.

When I reached him and helped him up, he said he didn't think he could make it to the bottom of the run.* By then, the rest of the family had reached the Togwotee Pass Traverse and were headed back to the Casper lift. Rather than calling the Ski Patrol for a courtesy sled, I asked the grandfather if he thought he could follow me through the stand of trees separating Wide Open from Sleeping Indian. I thought if he could manage to stay with me, we'd be able to traverse the Sleeping Indian run and ski directly to the Casper restaurant. He was willing to give it a try. He had to struggle a bit, but we succeeded in making our way through the stand of trees and over to the restaurant.

---

*   *In grandfather's defense, the run he encountered at Wide Open was more difficult than the run as it exists today. There have been significant changes to a number of ski runs at JHMR over the past two decades. Many of the changes have been made in an apparent attempt to attract more intermediate skiers and snowboarders to the mountain. An example of such an effort is the change made to Wide Open. A number of large boulders have been removed to eliminate the moguls and the run is now more inviting to intermediate skiers than it once was. The same has been done elsewhere and while it is not possible to alter the vertical pitch of the mountain, the ski resort has succeeded in smoothing out a number of runs to some degree in an effort to make portions of the mountain more accessible to average skiers. It also has upgraded old lifts and added new lefts, in some cases providing easy access to previously difficult areas to reach, which in the past were used primarily by locals.*

I left him there and skied down to his worried family at the base of the Casper lift. I told them grandad was waiting for them while having a cup of coffee in the restaurant and all they had to do was take the lift and ski down to join him. To this day I remember the surprised look on their faces.

There were other experiences that one would hope to avoid: dodging a loose snowboard careening down lower Gros Ventre in March when the terrain was strewn with ice balls and you had no idea where to stand to avoid being hit; being asked to carry a snowboard to the base of the mountain in high wind, causing it to act like a sail; and being hit from behind by a skier on lower Rendezvous Trail below the entrance to the Hobacks while giving a mountain tour to six people.

In that case, the skier knocked herself unconscious and as she lay in the snow I radioed Mountain Station to tell Ski Patrol that there was a skiing accident involving two people with one person, a young unconscious woman, needing a sled. I was asked whether the other skier involved was still at the scene and promptly responded that he was. We learned later she was trying to catch up to her husband and collided with me as I was making a turn.

Then there was the time we learned at our morning briefing that an out of town young male skier was missing at the end of the prior day, having been last seen at the top of Rendezvous Bowl. He had not turned up overnight. That morning I was assigned to the Sublette lift and spent my time searching for his body off Pepi's Run and the runs below Dog Face, only to learn around midday that two visiting skiers had spotted his body in a stand of trees below the trail leading from the top of the Sublette lift to the base of the bowl. Not being familiar with the terrain, he'd apparently come down skier's left of the bowl at a high rate of speed, flew across the trail and ended up partially covered with snow at the base of a tree.

I also vividly recall being at the top of the Thunder lift on January 28th, 2008 when severe weather and wind gusts around eighty miles an hour caused the mountain's entire lift system to shut down at 9:40 a.m. There was almost no visibility when I was asked by radio to make my way to the Bear Flats Snack Shack that existed at the time at the base of the Sublette lift and help any lost skiers on the way.

I felt my way over the Egg Carton and veered to my right, down Grand. The visibility was so poor, when trying to stand in one spot I became disoriented and had to sit in order to determine which way was down, then point my skis in that direction and let gravity take over. When I finally arrived, about thirty or so skiers and snowboarders who had been waiting at the base of the Sublette lift when the mountain was shut down had already crowded into the shack. After waiting in the shack for about an hour, I was told by radio to take the group down South Pass Traverse to the bottom of the mountain and, with the help of a snowboard instructor who was also sheltering in the shack, we managed to do so, led by the snow board instructor with me serving as sweep from the rear.

When we got to South Pass Traverse and Gros Ventre, the snowboard instructor and the group of skiers and snowboarders continued down lower GV, and I went on in the direction of the Casper restaurant.

As I made my way to the end of South Pass Traverse and to the base of the mountain, I found some skiers had abandoned their skis and tried to walk down. There were tree limbs and debris strewn around the mountain, people were disoriented, and in some cases injured. It was a mess.

Wednesday, January 6, 2010 was a tragic day on the mountain. As I recall, it snowed a lot the night before. After our morning host meeting at the MOB, a number of us skied down to the base of the mountain and were waiting to take lifts to our assigned areas when we heard on the radio that there would be a delay in opening the mountain to the public. Our job at that point was to be available to answer the usual questions regarding the reason for the delay.

The ski patrollers had been working to minimize any risk of an avalanche. While doing so, an avalanche was triggered just below Rendezvous Trail above Cheyenne Bowl and swept ski patroller Mark "Big Wally" Wolling off the cliff and buried him in about six feet of snow. He was dug out within ten minutes and was airlifted to Idaho in critical condition. The hosts knew from listening to radio exchanges between ski patrollers and Mountain Station that there was a serious problem, but it took a while before we knew how serious it was and who was involved.

Big Wally passed away three days later with family and friends at his side, including his longtime companion and my fellow Mountain Host, Marianne Hammersley, who was also working at the mountain that day and learned as we all did who the ski patroller was. Big Wally had a bigger than life personality and is now a legendary figure at JHMR. Fellow ski patrollers have marked the spot in Cheyenne Bowl where he was dug out of the avalanche with flags strung between two poles, and the forested area to skiers right of Cheyenne Bowl is now named Wally World. I remember little else that occurred while working as a Mountain Host that day.

Working as a host over the years, I continued to expand my knowledge and increase my appreciation of and respect for the mountain, discovering areas like the trees to skiers right of Rendezvous Trail below the entrance to the Hobacks when following Bill

Iams and his long-time skiing buddy, John Davies; unintentionally taking my friend and former partner Bob Pisano down Central Shoot; skiing Casper Traverse (known as "Mr. Toad's Wild Ride"), Casper Bowl and the traverse used by the Ski Patrol to access the top of the Casper lift; being caught in "Workers Wiggle" in the middle of Rendezvous Bowl and trying to stay upright until being spit out at the bottom; and trying to ski the runs off Dog Face, Flip Point and Dick's Ditch. Taking many of those runs for the first time was always a rush, but nothing seemed quite as challenging for me as that first year learning what it takes to become a Mountain Host.

From time to time I did sweeps at the end of the day at Après Vous and off the gondola, but I never had the opportunity to do another sweep off the tram. And I've never skied many of the well-known runs like Alta One (although I've assisted ski patrollers dealing with an injured skier near the bottom), the Expert Shoots, the Headwall (primarily because I didn't want to make the climb), or the runs beyond the ski resort boundary. After watching all the great young skiers on the mountain, I tended to believe that I started skiing too late in life, had diminished physical ability and stamina, was not a good enough skier, or had become too risk adverse to fully explore and take advantage of all the skiing opportunities offered at JHMR. As a consequence, I've never done or even seriously considered skiing Corbet's Couloir. When asked from time to time by out of town skiers if I had, I've always adopted the response given by my departed friend and former law partner, Mike Hammer, one of the best looking skiers I've ever had the pleasure of following down the slopes. Mike's response was simply, "I've never felt the need."

For many years JHMR has had ski groups like the "Old Dogs" who enjoy having first tracks ahead of the general public. I became a member of the "Thursday Thunder Ski Group" with Jim Russell as the instructor. The group included Bill Iams, Peter Ordway, Ken Taylor, Richard Laumeyer, and Gail and Monte Kvittem. To this day, I still remember Jim's seven P's – "Proper Prior Planning Prevents Piss Poor Performance." Later, I formed the "Skiaholics" with Lowell Martindale, Bob Pisano, Mike Hammer, Vicki Henderson, Brent Backman, and Eddie Kolsky as our instructor. Among other things, he taught us "the move," how best to turn on steep terrain.

Before the host party at the end of the 2011-2012 season, Bill Hoglund and I talked about how impressed we were with Lee Ann's leadership and he suggested we do something to commemorate her achievements. I gave it some thought and arranged to have a plaque made in her honor as the outstanding leader of the Jackson Hole Mountain Hosts. The plaque attempted to capture the essence of what she means to the program, and I presented it to her at the Mountain Host party held at the old Wilson Schoolhouse:

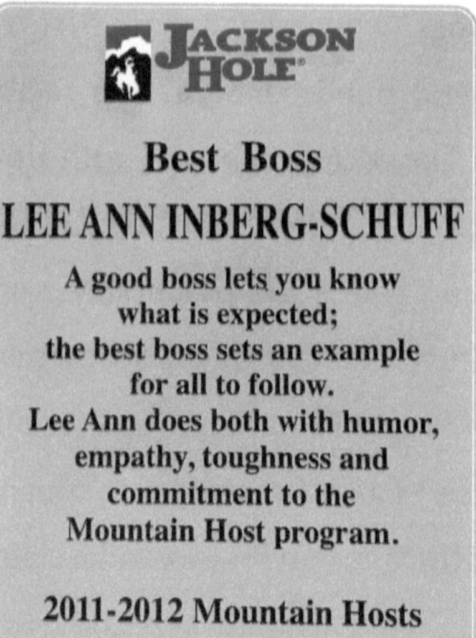

I also arranged to have a second plaque made which was intended to capture my notion of an important element of being a successful Mountain Host. I gave that plaque to her the following day.

Barbara joined the Mountain Host team as a non-ski host a year after I'd become a Mountain Host and continued in that role for an additional four years after I left the program. The experience volunteering at JHMR has been one of the most rewarding either of us has had since making Jackson Hole our home.

Four outstanding Mountain Hosts, Paul Vogelheim, Bill Hoglund, Sally Berman and Joel Berman, enjoying lunch at the gondola Mountain Host desk in January 2014.

Barbara, Bill and their God-daughter, Tess Elliott from Australia, at the top of the gondola with Corbet's Couloir in the background in December 2014.

A recovering former Mountain Host: August 2021 photo of Bill and his spine surgeon, Dr. Burak Ozgur, Director of the Hoag Spine Center.